THE
BEST
AMERICAN
POETRY
1997

◇   ◇   ◇

James Tate, Editor

David Lehman, Series Editor

SCRIBNER POETRY

SCRIBNER POETRY
SCRIBNER
1230 Avenue of the Americas
New York, NY 10020

SCRIBNER POETRY and design are trademarks of Simon & Schuster Inc.

Set in Bembo

Manufactured in the United States of America

1   3   5   7   9   10   8   6   4   2

ISBN 0-684-81452-8
ISSN 1040-5763

CONTENTS

David Lehman was born in New York City in 1948. He attended Cambridge University as a Kellett Fellow and went on to receive his doctorate in English at Columbia University, where he was Lionel Trilling's research assistant. He is the author of three books of poems, including *Valentine Place* (Scribner, 1996) and *Operation Memory* (Princeton, 1990). His prose books include *Signs of the Times: Deconstruction and the Fall of Paul de Man* and *The Big Question.* He is the general editor of the University of Michigan Press's Poets on Poetry Series and is on the core faculty of the graduate writing programs at Bennington College and the New School for Social Research. He also teaches at Columbia. He divides his time between Ithaca, New York, and New York City.

FOREWORD

by David Lehman

◊ ◊ ◊

Every force creates a counter-force, and the ballyhooed recent resurgence of American poetry has been no exception. For every CNN report touting the "spoken word" scene, hip-hop poems, and poetry slams, a dour voice has piped up that it is not amused. There are those, there have always been those, who contend that what is new is meretricious and what is old, irrelevant. A vague dissatisfaction with what contemporary American poetry has to offer is a staple of Sunday book supplements. Rather than printing a review of a new poetry book each week, the editors salve their consciences by running a semiannual story about the uncertain fate of poetry in the era of the internet or about how writing programs make for mediocre verse. The more self-examining of the plaintiffs wonder whether poetry is a thing of youth, and it is the poetry of their youth—the poetry they read in college—to which they pledge their fealty. It's as if a teenage crush on Mickey Mantle had incapacitated the fan from appreciating the skills of Ken Griffey, Jr.

The standard-issue article about poetry's problems is a temptation for essayists who realize that few actual poems need to be read in order to accomplish the task. They can vent their nostalgia for the Romantic period, when poets had the good sense to die young, and their annoyance with versifiers who refuse to shut up though they have sixty or more winters on their heads. A new volume every three years is seen not as heartening evidence of poetic longevity but as the unfortunate side effect of academic necessity. Too many poems are "competent"—an odd complaint, and one that nobody would think to apply disdainfully to short stories or essays. But then perhaps we expect better, a higher standard of excellence, and not only excellence but inspiration, from poets than we do from our other writers.

It is the nature of most criticism to be sour. John Updike publishes a book every season? The critics say he writes too much. Thomas Pynchon writes too little. Poets, however, can't write little enough. No one held it against Philip Larkin that he wrote one good poem in his last dry decade. (There were complaints enough about his xenophobia and sexism.) Poetry is too personal, or it is not personal enough. Rhyme and meter are old hat, yet poems lacking them are slack. More people are writing poetry than ever before, but little of it will last. More than twelve hundred poetry titles have been published annually in the United States since 1993, but that merely reverses a precipitous decline—from nearly thirteen hundred a year to just under nine hundred—in the aftermath of the stock market crash in October 1987. Poetry's ghetto is in the back of the bookshop far from the cash register. But poetry had better not pitch its tent where there are lights and cameras, since popular poetry is a contradiction in terms.

Critics inveigh against poetry writing programs on the grounds that they turn out mostly poetasters and epigones. The same critics forget that the fruits of an arts education begin with the ability to appreciate the art in question. If the lampooned institution of the creative writing workshop creates the readership of the future, more power to it. We do not consider the student of Plato to be a failure if he does not produce a dialogue of the quality of the *Symposium*. Nor should the likelihood of failure stand in the way of making the effort. Sometimes a spectacular failure is worth any number of modest successes. The study of writing would seem as important an experience for the professional scholar or general reader as for the aspiring writer, and it would be difficult to exaggerate the part that workshops can play, for good or ill, in creating the taste by which our poetry will be enjoyed. It is a profound irony that skills at reading poetry, which once were taught in English departments, now owe their existence to writing workshops, where literature rather than metatextual theorizing remains in favor.

For the second straight year, a poet won the Nobel Prize for literature. The announcement on October 3 that Wislawa Szymborska of Poland had won the 1996 award vaulted her from obscurity to international prominence overnight. Editors and journalists scrambled to find Szymborska's work and commissioned translators to render it into English. By a splendid coincidence that illustrated Gertrude Stein's sense of the word ("a coincidence is something that is going to happen, and does"), both *The New Republic* and *The New Yorker* printed the same Szymborska poem on the same October week in two different translations. "Some People Like Poetry," as translated by Stanislaw Baranczak and Clare Cavanagh, was the version that ran in *The New Republic*. It ended this way:

Poetry—
but what is poetry anyway?
More than one rickety answer
has tumbled since that question first was raised.
But I just keep on not knowing, and I cling to that
like a redemptive handrail.

"Some Like Poetry," Joanna Trzeciak's version in *The New Yorker*, arrived at a different conclusion:

Poetry—
but what sort of thing is poetry?
More than one shaky answer
has been given to this question.
But I do not know and do not know and clutch on to it,
as to a saving bannister.

In Trzeciak's translation, poetry is the bannister that helps the poet keep her balance on the vertiginous staircase of unknowing. In the Baranczak/Cavanagh translation, not poetry but the poet's determination to persist in the absence of certainties and facts is what is redemptive. So profound is the difference that the concurrent appearance of the two translations seemed itself to constitute a literary event—an ambiguous parable that could yield lessons ranging from the familiar ("poetry is what is lost in translation") to the paradoxical ("poetry is mistranslation"). What was not in dispute was the fact that Szymborska's work had begun to attract the attention and admiration that may not be essential to the writing of poetry but are surely a grace for all who read and love it.

Perhaps because of the official presidential designation of April as National Poetry Month, the first line of "The Waste Land" provided the lead for more soft-news stories in 1996 than in any past year, and the rest of the poem received its due when the British actress Fiona Shaw presented it in a one-woman show at a suitably dilapidated off-Broadway theater in November. In general, National Poetry Month received a good press, though some of the articles mixed their metaphors with wince-provoking abandon ("Poetry is a bomb that frags you with metaphor, explodes in your head where it heals rather than harms," wrote one enthusiast). As a gimmick, if that's what it is, National Poetry Month worked, stimulating a proliferation of readings, lectures, and bookstore events related to poetry. Sales were up by 35 percent at Borders and 25 percent at Barnes & Noble. Independent bookstores like the Hungry Mind in Saint Paul, Minnesota, did even better. In Los Angeles, the UCLA Bookstore reported an increase of "at least 600%" with $3,500 in poetry receipts in the first week of April alone. To mark the second appearance of National Poetry Month, in 1997, thousands of free copies of "The Waste Land" were distributed at U.S. post offices on April 15, the cruelest day of all.

Not everyone was charmed, however. Richard Howard, a chancellor of the Academy of American Poets, the organization that initiated National Poetry Month, said, "I was never before so certain why April was declared by a poet to be the cruelest month; now I know." He had "no hesitation" in calling National Poetry Month "the worst thing to have happened to poetry since the advent of the camera and the internal combustion engine, two inventions which the poet Wystan Auden once declared to be the bane of our modernity." In Mr. Howard's view, such a ploy as National Poetry Month cannot but contribute to the commodification of poetry, putting the art on a par with the chocolates and flowers customarily purchased on Valentine's Day. The workings of capitalism have sanitized poetry when the thing to do is to eroticize it. "So wretched, and so absurd, has the position of poetry writing become in our polity—unread though occasionally exhibited, despised though invariably ritualized, as at certain inaugurations—that not only are we determined to put the poor thing out of its agony, but we have made it a patriotic duty to do so." Publicity, in an age of publicity, was an enemy. Let us, Mr. Howard urged, "make poetry, once again, a secret."

Poetry always was a secret pleasure, indulged in alone, the self communing with a book as the writer of that book once communed alone with the cosmos. Something has changed, as Mr. Howard notes, in an age of consumerism, sophisticated marketing techniques, advanced communications technology, and television's vast wasteland. Poetry readings have, to an extent unforeseen when Dylan Thomas and Allen Ginsberg were the rage, replaced the solitary act of reading. Poetry is more of a group event than it used to be. At least that is the public aspect of poetry—the poetry that is most visible and audible. Compare the poetry of today with that of a quarter century ago and you see a sharp rise in the number of public poems: not that they necessarily deal with public issues, just that they seem to have been written with a live audience, ready to sigh on cue, in the poet's mind.

But it is the nature of secrets to avoid being found out, and the clamor and din surrounding poetry do not deny that something important may be happening far from the spotlight. What is this news, and how is it to be found out? If it is up to posterity to determine the lasting value of works of art, on what basis can we anticipate the process today? If we are to begin to judge, however tentatively and falteringly, who is to do the selecting?

The Best American Poetry has, since its inception nine volumes ago, made available to an increasing readership a wide and generous sampling of the poems of our time. From the start we have felt that an annual winnowing was essential, since no casual reader can possibly keep up with all the poetry that is published annually in periodicals and since a surprisingly high proportion of those poems are worth reading more than once. A test of good poetry is that it compel multiple rereadings, and that is certainly a test that the editors of *The Best American Poetry* have taken to heart. Our period, as even cranky critics note, is rich in poets who have had long and productive careers. The guest editors of this anthology come from these distinguished ranks. They are asked to be as ecumenical as they can be, but it is always understood that each will honor his or her own lights. The result is, in effect, a work-in-progress, for *The Best American Poetry* is meant to provide a continuing record of the taste and judgment of our leading poets. It is also meant to heed the imperative articulated by Wallace Stevens: "It must give pleasure."

I asked James Tate to edit *The Best American Poetry 1997,* not only because I admire his writing but because I know him to be a discriminating reader and I was curious to see what poems he would deem fittest to survive. Born in Kansas City, Missouri, in 1943, Mr. Tate burst on the poetry scene in 1966 when his book *The Lost Pilot* was chosen for the Yale Younger Poets Series. He was among the youngest ever to achieve that distinction. His *Selected Poems,* a distillation of his first nine volumes, won the Pulitzer Prize for poetry in 1992. In 1995 he received the Dorothea Tanning Award from the Academy of American Poets. In addition to his poems, he has written short stories, and he is the co-author, with Bill Knott, of a terrific book of collaborative poems improbably titled *Are You Ready, Mary Baker Eddy?* (1970).

While *The Best American Poetry 1997* naturally reflects Mr. Tate's predilections as a poet, I think the reader will find that the contents are as unpredictable as the plot twists in a French prose poem. Poems were selected from thirty-nine magazines, with *Poetry* topping the list (eight selections), followed by *The American Poetry Review* (six), *Ploughshares* and *The New Republic* (five apiece). The book is strong on narrative—what one poet calls the "stories in poetry." There are a number of prose poems, but there are also prayers and meditations and chants, a poem in the form of a fan letter and a *sui generis* poem in the form of haiku-like bumper stickers. The music in the background is provided by Mozart, Beethoven, Wagner, Gershwin, Mick Jagger, Janis Joplin, Bob Dylan, and the Sex Pistols. Among the subjects addressed are "the problem of anxiety," "the exaggeration of despair," and whether History to the survivors may say alas but cannot help or pardon. In one poem we find Jesus, Mary, and Joseph and in the next one Groucho, Beppo, and Harpo. Little Red Riding Hood, Clytemnestra, and Sisyphus put in appearances. The poets think about thinking, smoking, bourbon, heroin, California, death, and the sexes, their chronic conflicts and periodic acts of reconciliation. The anthology includes the work of four recently deceased poets—Joseph Brodsky, William Dickey, Allen Ginsberg, and Larry Levis—mourned and honored here.

When James Tate's most recent collection, *Worshipful Company of Fletchers* (Ecco Press), won the 1994 National Book Award in poetry, the citation began as follows: "A reader of James Tate's poetry, laughing out loud, said, 'I didn't know that poetry was allowed to be so much fun.' " We hope that the poems in this volume will provoke a similarly delighted response. If poetry is its own excuse for being, as Emerson said of beauty, there can be no defense of it more eloquent than verse.

> Articles about the dismal state of poetry
> Bemoan the absence of form and meter or,
> Conversely, the products of "forms workshop":
> Dream sonnets, sestinas based on childhood photographs,
> Eclogues set in Third Avenue bars,
> Forms contrived to suit an emergent occasion.
> God knows it's easy enough to mock our enterprise,
> Hard, though, to succeed at it, since
> It sometimes seems predicated on failure.
> Just when the vision appears, an importunate
> Knock on the door banishes it, and you
> Lethe-wards have sunk, or when a sweet
> Melancholic fit should transport you to a
> North Pole of absolute concentration,
> Obligations intrude, putting an end to the day's

Poem. Poetry like luck is the residue of
Quirky design, and it
Refreshes like a soft drink full of bubbles
Sipped in a stadium on a lazy August afternoon
That was supposed to be spent at a boring job.
Ultimately poetry is
Virtue if it is our lot to choose, err, regret and
Wonder why in speech that would melt the stars.
X marks the spot of
Your latest attempt. Point at a map, blindfolded:
Zanzibar. Shall we go there, you and I?

James Tate was born in Kansas City, Missouri, in 1943. In 1966, when he won the Yale Younger Poets Prize for his first book, *The Lost Pilot,* he was among the youngest poets ever thus honored. His *Selected Poems* (Wesleyan/University Press of New England, 1991) was awarded the Pulitzer Prize for poetry in 1992, and his most recent book, *Worshipful Company of Fletchers* (Ecco Press), won the National Book Award two years later. Other collections by James Tate include *Constant Defender* (Ecco Press, 1983), *Reckoner* (Wesleyan University Press, 1986), and *Distance from Loved Ones* (Wesleyan/University Press of New England, 1990). He has written short fiction and has completed a manuscript under the working title *Forty-five Stories.* In 1995 he was awarded the Dorothea Tanning Award from the Academy of American Poets. Since 1971 he has taught at the University of Massachusetts. He lives in Amherst.

INTRODUCTION

by James Tate

◇　◇　◇

Like it or not, we are a part of our time. We speak the language of our time. For poets, it may be more rarefied; it may be more adorned or convoluted, but, nonetheless, in some way it is reflective of our culture. I, for instance, as a very young man, was relieved when I first read William Carlos Williams and I realized I could stop trying to write like Algernon Swinburne.

I know I am not alone when I confess that I have stared at a blank sheet of paper for hours, day after day. Why? Why is it so difficult? Because I want to travel to a new place. Not only do I want the language to be new, I also want the ideas to be new. I want the whole world to be new! We know that that is impossible, but desire is not rational.

Well, we know Columbus did not set sail for America. But what he got was not so bad. We concentrate all we know into the moment, with some fearful peeping into the near future. When I make the mistake of imagining how a whole poem should unfold, I immediately want to destroy that plan. Nothing should supplant the true act of discovery.

The poem is like a very demanding but beautiful pet. It says, "I want this. No, I don't want that. Now I need this, and more of that. But I don't want any of that," and so on. Corrective move. Wanting both truth and beauty, the beauty of language in pursuit of truth.

Some poems want to do their work in the quietest way, like a spider working in a corner. Others are very noisy, banging words against one another as if they were tin cans. One kind of poem is not inherently better than another.

Amazingly, year after year, surprising, subtle, profound, funny, and sad new poems are written and published. Poems we could not have imagined; poems we now know we needed. There is no end to our needing poetry. Without poetry our Culture and, more importantly, our collective Spirit, would be a tattered, wayward thing.

The daily routine of our lives can be good and even wonderful, but there is still a hunger in us for the mystery of the deep waters, and poetry can fulfill that hunger. It speaks to that place in us that seems incomplete. And it can assure us that we are not crazy or alone, and that is a tall order.

What we want from poetry is to be moved, to be moved from where we now stand. We don't just want to have our ideas or emotions confirmed. Or if we do, then we turn to lesser poems, poems that tell you killing children is bad, chopping down the rainforest is bad, dying is sad. A good poet would agree with all of those sentiments, but would also strive for an understanding beyond those givens.

The poet arrives at his or her discovery by setting language on edge or creating metaphors that suggest dangerous ideas, or any number of other methods. The point is, language can be hazardous as it is our primary grip on the world. When language is skewed, the world is viewed differently. But this is only effective if the reader can recognize this view, even though it is the first time he or she has experienced the thought.

When you come upon a poem you especially like, what separates it from so many other well-made poems is the quality of its insight. And for this word "insight" I would happily substitute the loftier words "revelation" or "epiphany."

Style and voice serve as a means of seduction. They are the rites of courting. They help create the appropriate tone and ambiance and set of possibilities whereby the revelation may occur. I say "may" because there are no guarantees. The poet can only hope for it. Revelations known beforehand are by definition not revelations.

The act of writing poetry is a search for the unknown. Each line written is searching for the next line. And as the weight, the length, of the poem accumulates, so too does the pressure accumulate for a revelation to occur. Each image or idea should point the way to another image or idea. And each of these indicates the need for further development if the poem is to achieve its maximum potential. Each poem dictates the magnitude of the revelation. An extremely small insight can be satisfying. Simply offering the reader a new way of seeing a common object or familiar experience qualifies as an insight or epiphany. Charles Simic *begins* a poem called "Fork" like this:

> This strange thing must have Crept
> Right out of hell.
> It resembles a bird's foot
> Worn around the cannibal's neck.

We are in a provocative, new world from the get-go, but also one that the reader can immediately see.

It is very clear, when reading Ovid or John Clare or Edna St. Vincent Millay or John Ashbery, that human beings don't change. Their circumstances, their life expectancies, and, yes, their languages change, but their emotions do not. Their joys, their heartaches, their griefs, their jealousies, etc., are remarkably the same as they were two thousand years ago. Still, poets persist in penetrating the mysteries surrounding our condition and enlivening our language while doing so.

Writing a poem is like traversing an obstacle course or negotiating a maze. Or downhill skiing. We tell ourselves, for the sake of excitement, to up the ante, that the choices we make could prove fatal. Anything to help us get where we must go, wherever the hell that is. When poets are actually working, theorizing is the last thing they have time for.

Once the poem is heated up and seems to be going someplace exciting, there is very little the poet would not do to insure its arrival. And of course it is always supposed to appear easy and natural. (About as natural as baking a live yak pie.)

Some fine poems are written in one sitting; others take a year or more. That doesn't seem to matter. Just as it doesn't matter if they are written with lipstick on the back end of a pig. It doesn't matter if they are written about a mite or the end of the world. One of the things that matters is the relationship of all the parts and elements of the poem to each other. Is everything working toward the same goal? Is there anything extraneous? Or if there is some kind of surface disunity, can that be justified by some larger purpose?

Why is it that you can't just take some well-written prose, divide it into lines, and call it poetry? (Thank you for asking that question, you jerk.) While most prose is a kind of continuous chatter, describing, naming, explaining, poetry speaks against an essential backdrop of silence. It is almost reluctant to speak at all, knowing that it can never fully name what is at the heart of its intention. There is a prayerful, haunted silence between words, between phrases, between images, ideas and lines. This is one reason why good poems can be read over and over. The reader, perhaps without knowing it, instinctively desires to peer between the cracks into the other world where the unspoken rests in darkness.

Well-meaning friends and colleagues are forever offering me ideas for poems, bizarre scenes they've witnessed or comic ideas they themselves have hatched. Thankless creature that I am, I've never even been tempted to take advantage of these gifts. And when I was young I had the idea that if I was going to make a go of it as a poet I had better get out there in the world and have some big adventures so that I would have something to write about. And I did go out there and seek big adventures and found them aplenty. Sad to report not one of them ever found its way into a poem, not even a little bit. And so, too, today, a certain bird is more likely to find its way into a poem of mine than a train wreck I witnessed.

Is it that the train wreck speaks for itself, announces its tragedy so clearly, whereas the bird is subtle and can evoke a thousand possible suggestions? These are rather bald-faced examples. What I was trying to address is how the poet arrives at his or her "subject matter." First of all, it doesn't really "arrive," and secondly, most poets would tell you that the phrase "subject matter" is inappropriate when discussing poetry. All the elements of the poem make the poem, are the poem. You cannot extricate "subject matter" from them, unless you really believe that clothes make the man.

For me sometimes a poem at its most preliminary stage may begin by sensing texture. I walk around for hours wondering what this texture is and if I can find one or two words that would approximate its essence. Admittedly, this is a very slow way to start a poem, but it is one that has got me going many times. It is one that has opened doors that would have otherwise gone ignored. But these one or two words will then point the way to a few more, until eventually ideas and images come trickling or flooding in.

When one is highly alert to language, then nearly everything begs to be in a poem—words overheard on a subway or in a supermarket, graffiti, newspaper headlines, a child's school lesson blowing down the street. This is the most exciting state to be in. Commonplace words are suddenly mysterious and beautiful. Someone uses a phrase "baby farm," and your head spins with delight. "Savoy cabbage," "fine-tooth comb," "patrol wagon," it doesn't matter how mundane when the poet, almost beyond his or her control, is seeking language, questioning it, testing it. The poet will take that commonplace piece of language and "make it new."

In my experience poets are not different from other people. You have your dullards, your maniacs, your mild eccentrics, etc. Except for this one thing they do—write poems. And in this they are singularly strange. They may end up with an audience and a following of some sort, but in truth they write their poems with various degrees of obsessiveness mostly for themselves, for the pleasure and satisfaction it gives them. And for the hunger and need nothing else can abate.

And then, if given the chance, most are happy to publish their finished work, and, likewise, if given the chance, they are happy to read their poems in public and accept, perhaps even bask in, any applause that might be forthcoming. And for that moment it may appear that the poet is in complete command of his or her faculties, and that he or she wrote these poems with this kind of audience in mind. And at that moment the poet may even believe it. But fortunately this is not true. I say "fortunately" because if it were true then poetry would only be a kind of entertainment. It is precisely because the poet has written his poems in solitude for himself to satisfy unanalyzable hungers and to please his highest standards with negligible prospects of any other rewards that the poem is incorruptible and may address issues unaddressed by many people in their daily lives. Therefore, when people hear or read this poem they may, just may, respond eagerly and take heart at hearing or reading what they themselves have never been able to utter, but now suspect is true. I suspect that if the poet were to pander to his audience not much new would ever get said.

And it seems we are equally grateful for the serious and dark poem as for those that amuse us. This anthology has many of both kinds, and all shades in between. There is a very large and wonderfully diverse company of poets at work out there in America. This anthology is but a small reflection, and lacks many of my favorite poets. On the other hand, there were many discoveries for me, poets I had not heard of at all, poets whom I had not paid enough attention to before.

Now, after an exhilarating year of reading, it is time to say: Go, little book, make some friends if you can.

THE
BEST
AMERICAN
POETRY
1997

◇ ◇ ◇

Back in the World

◊ ◊ ◊

I took a shortcut through blood
to get back to you,
but the house where I left you is empty now.
You've packed up and moved on,
leaving this old photograph of the two of us,
taken before I left for Viet Nam.
You've cut yourself out of it,
torn your half in pieces
and lain them on the mantel,
where your knickknacks used to be:
those godawful Hummels you'd been saving for years
and a small glass vial you said
contained your grandmother's tears.
A thick film of dust comes off on my fingers,
when I rub them across the years
that came to separate us.

In a corner of the living room, facing a wall,
I find my last painting of you.
In it, you lie, naked, on the old iron bed,
your head hanging over the side,
your hair, flowing to the floor
like a wide black river.
There, Max, the cat, is curled
in a grey, purring blur,
all fur and gooseberry green eyes that stare at me,
as if accusing me of some indiscretion
he doesn't dare mention.
Suddenly, he meows loudly

and rises as if he's been spooked,
runs through the house,
then swoops back to his place beside you,
and beside the night table,
on which I've painted a heart on a white plate,
and a knife and fork on a red checkered napkin.
You hate the painting. You say I'm perverse
to paint you that way, and worse, an amateur.

"Do you want to tear my heart out and eat it
like those Aztecs used to do,
so you can prove you don't need me?" you ask.
"But I do need you," I say. "That's the point."
"I don't get it," you say,
as you dress for some party
you claim you are going to, but I'm on to your game.
It's your lover who's waiting for you.
"I know who he is," I say,
"but I don't know his name,"
then I run to the bathroom,
grab a handful of Trojans
and throw them at you,
as you slam the door on me,
before I can slam it on you.
You don't come back, until you get word
that I've enlisted in the army.
I'm packing when you show up.
"You heard," I say
and you tell me that it's perverse of me too.
"Who are you kidding, you, a soldier?
And what's that?" you ask.
I give you the small canvas I've just finished.
"A sample of my new work," I say.
"There's nothing on it," you say.
"That's right," I tell you. "It's white like the plate,
after I ate your heart."
"Don't start," you say, "don't."
We part with a brief kiss like two strangers
who miss the act of pressing one mouth
against another, yet resist, resist.

We part on a day just like this,
a day that seems as if it will never end,
in an explosion that sends my body
flying through the air
in the white glare of morning,
when without warning, I step on a landmine
and regain consciousness to find
I'm a notation on a doctor's chart that says,
BK amputee.

Now I imagine myself racing through the house
just as Max did once,
only to return to myself, to the bed,
the night table, the canvas in my lap
and my brush, poised above it.
When Max, toothless and so old,
his hair comes out in clumps, when I touch him,
half sits, half collapses beside my wheelchair,
I begin to paint, first a black background,
then starting from the left side,
a white line, beside a red line
beside a white, beside a red,
each one getting smaller and smaller,
until they disappear off the edge of the canvas.
I title it "Amateur."
I call it art.

from *Quarterly West*

The Exaggeration of Despair

◊   ◊   ◊

I open the door

(this Indian girl writes that her brother tried to hang himself
with a belt just two weeks after her other brother did hang himself

and this Indian man tells us that, back in boarding school, five priests
took him into a back room and raped him repeatedly

and this homeless Indian woman begs for quarters, and when I ask
her about the tribe, she says she's horny and bends over in front of me

and this Indian brother dies in a car wreck on the same road
as his older brother, his youngest brother, and the middle brother

and this homeless Indian man is the uncle of an Indian man
who writes for a large metropolitan newspaper, and so I know them both

and this Indian child cries when he sits to eat at our table
because he had never known his family to sit at the same table

and this Indian poet shivers beneath the freeway
and begs for enough quarters to buy a pencil and paper

and this fancydancer passes out at the powwow
and wakes up naked, with no memory of the evening, all of his regalia gone

and this is my sister, who waits years for an eagle, receives it
and stores it with our cousins, who then tell her it has disappeared

and this is my father, whose own father died on Okinawa, shot
by a Japanese soldier who must have looked so much like him

and this is my father, whose mother died of tuberculosis
not long after he was born, and so my father must hear coughing ghosts

and this is my grandmother who saw, before the white men came,
three ravens with white necks, and knew our God was going to change)

and invite the wind inside.

from *Urbanus*

Return to Harmony 3

◇ ◇ ◇

Two summers? Epochs, then, of ice.

But the air is the same muslin, beaten by the sky on Nanga Parbat, then pressed on the rocks of the nearer peaks.

I run down the ramp.

On the tarmac, I eavesdrop on Operation Tiger: Troops will burn down the garden and let the haven remain.

This is home—the haven a cage surrounded by ash—the fate of Paradise.

Through streets strewn with broken bricks and interrupted by para-militaries, Irfan drives me straight to the Harmonies ("3" for my father—the youngest brother!), three houses built in a pastoral, that walled acreage of Harmonies where no one but my mother was poor.

A bunker has put the house under a spell. Shadowed eyes watch me open the gate, like a trespasser.

Has the gardener fled?

The Annexe of the Harmonies is locked—my grandmother's cottage—where her sons offered themselves to her as bouquets of mirrors. There was nothing else to reflect.

Under the windows the roses have choked in their beds. Was the gardener killed?

And the postman?

In the drawer of the cedar stand peeling in the verandah, a pile of damp letters—one to my father to attend a meeting the previous autumn, another an invitation to a wedding.

My first key opens the door. I break into quiet. The lights work.

The Koran still protects the house, lying strangely wrapped in a *jamawar* shawl where my mother had left it on the walnut table by the fireplace. Above, *If God is with you, Victory is near!*—the framed calligraphy ruthless behind cobwebs.

I pick up the dead phone, its number exiled from its instrument, a refugee among forlorn numbers in some angry office on Exchange Road.

But the receiver has caught a transmission: Rafi's song from a film about war: *Slowly, I so slowly, kept on walking, / and then was severed forever from her.* THIS IS ALL INDIA RADIO, AMRITSAR. I hang up.

Upstairs, the window too is a mirror; if I jump through it I will fall into my arms.

The mountains return my stare, untouched by blood.

On my shelf, by Ritsos and Rilke and Cavafy and Lorca and Iqbal and Amichai and Paz, my parents are beautiful in their wedding brocades, so startlingly young!

And there in black and white my mother, eighteen years old, a year before she came a bride to these Harmonies, so unforgivenly poor and so unforgivingly beautiful that the house begins to shake in my arms, and when the unarmed world is still again, with pity, it is the house that is holding me in its arms and the cry coming faded from its empty rooms is my cry.

from *Verse*

31

From *Strip*

◇ ◇ ◇

1.

wdn't it be silly to be serious, now:
I mean, the hardheads and the eggheads

are agreed that we are an absurd
irrelevance on this slice of curvature

and that a boulder from the blue
could confirm it: imagine, mathematics

wiped out by a wandering stone, or
Grecian urns not forever fair when

the sun expands: can you imagine
cracking the story off we've built

up so long—the simian ancestries,
the lapses and leaps, the discovery

of life in the burial of grains:
the scratch of pictorial and syllabic

script, millennia of evenings around
the fires: nothing: meaninglessness

our only meaning: our deepest concerns
such as death or love or child-pain

arousing a belly laugh or a witty
dismissal: a bunch of baloney: it's

already starting to feel funny: I
think I may laugh: few of the dead

lie recalled, and they have not
cautioned us: we are rippers and

tearers and proceeders: restraint
stalls us still—we stand hands

empty, lip hung, dumb eyes struck
open: if we can't shove at the

trough, we don't understand: but is
it not careless to become too local

when there are four hundred billion
stars in our galaxy alone: at

least, that's what I heard: also,
that there are billions of such

systems spread about, some older,
some younger than ours: if the

elements are the elements throughout,
I daresay much remains to be learned:

however much we learn, tho, we may
grow daunted by our dismissibility

in so sizable a place: do our gods
penetrate those reaches, or do all

those other places have their godly
nativities: or if the greatest god

is the stillness all the motions add
up to, then we must ineluctably be

included: perhaps a dribble of
what-is is what what-is is: it is

nice to be included, especially from
so minor a pew: please turn, in yr

hymnals, to page "Archie carrying on
again:" he will have it his way

though he has no clue what his way
is: after such participation as

that with the shrill owl in the
spruce at four in the morning with

the snow ended and the moon come
out, how am I sagely to depart from

all being (universe and all—by
that I mean material and immaterial

stuff) without calling out—just a
minute, am I not to know at last

what lies over the hill: over the
ridge there, over the laps of the

ocean, and out beyond the plasmas
of the sun's winds, and way out

where the bang still bubbles in the
longest risings: no, no: I must

get peanut butter and soda crackers
and the right shoe soles (for ice)

and leave something for my son and
leave these lines, poor things, to

you, if you will have them, can they
do you any good, my trade for my

harm in the world: come, let's
celebrate: it will all be over

from *The Paris Review*

That Cold Summer

◇   ◇   ◇

At first the angel was perfectly wingless,
loitering out in the meadow below our summer place,

gazing up at the sky. A kind of Christina
without a home behind her. Whenever she was hungry,

she'd sneak into our home and steal an apple
or a peach from the walnut bowl. Once she cracked a tooth

on a porcelain grape and bled a milky light,
moaning softly while the white stuff circled her forehead

like a pie plate. Donald didn't believe it, thinking
she was just another of his crazy imaginings,

not being one to listen much to his own eyes.
Back then he mistook angel blood for a halo.

Approaching her gingerly, he looked into her pale eyes,
afraid to speak, informing me just how airy

she was, like a piece of the sky looking at herself.
She watched him like a deer caught in headlights, staring

until he touched her shoulder, and he shuddered.
Colder than snow, she was. Donald said that's why

he invited her in to warm herself. She had a long
wind inside her that fanned the flames a brilliant blue.

Personally, I didn't care for her antics,
but Donald was enchanted. Had I ever laid eyes

on a thing like that? he'd ask. As if making gales
in my home were a miracle or something. Once

I woke to find her sleeping in the silence beside me,
her legs spread wide as a crooked smile, the white

mist leaking out in a stream. The icy draft
in our bed lasted for weeks. At first I hardly noticed

the feathers slipping into cracks in the floor,
the shopping bags and the soup I kept simmering

on the stove, feathers swimming like dust in the window
light, tiny white feathers with lives of their own

like those brine shrimp they sell at drugstores
to gullible children. When the feathers

became more plentiful and blew around the rooms,
I swept them out the door, and they rose and drifted

like earthbound clouds. The angel was soon nowhere
to be seen, though her shadow spread, even grew to tower

over us. Those must have been huge wings sprouting
from her shoulders. For me, it couldn't have come

soon enough. Though the house, afterwards, was of a sudden
so familiar and empty, I often wondered how she flew.

from *Ploughshares*

L . S . A S E K O F F

Rounding the Horn

◇ ◇ ◇

I was a week away from the red chip when they outed me from
      Gay AA
for phonesex in the detox closet, swilling bottles of phony
      cologne—*Esprit,*
bootlegged by my bunkmate, a walleyed cowboy from Melville,
      Long Island.
Brothers, Sisters, I said, cursed from birth with a terrible thirst
      by the Dreaded Enabler
who bent my elbow at the Brazen Head bar, nursed bitter milk
      from barrels at Baileys,
I was born of a triple-Virgo by the blind porter at World's End,
the black Irish Jewish Catholic alcoholic offspring of
that lost tribe of penmen, those heinous sheenies & Arab
      seamen, Shawn & Shem.
Or, as they say in Mayo, to make a short story malinger, Once I
      drank to stop the voices,
now I drink to bring them back. At which point Schein turned to
      Schauer with a sour grin,
Dollink, tell me, vy iz Cleo's noze zo long? Becawz, my deeah,
      she'z de qveen ov de Nial!

Locked on the mountaintop with all the 12-steppers & those
      jovial overweight
Franciscan friars whose strict diet condemns them to die at 50 of
      beer & potatoes,
I was sore all over as though fallen from a great height
with a hollow ache in the blades at my back where the wings
      once were.

Kneeling before the porcelain bowl I saw a ghost-face flower
        haloed by my fiery orange hair
& someone had lipsticked across the glass roof of Hell: NO
        BUDY LUVS NO ONE.
That's when the statues started talking back to me . . .

Grand Rounds. Doctor Glanders illuminates a map of the dark
        side of the moon—
its rilles & furrows & lunar seas. Weighing each word on his
        tongue like a turd on a golden scale,
he points toward me. This lad has the brain of an 80 year old
        man!
With all due respect, I reply, you are not addressing some
        riverboat queen
with a taste for pink magnolias & scarlet cock. See the pearl in
        this left ear?
I got it rounding the Horn in rough trade, foul weather, lashed
        to the mast,
loony as a snowbird, wailing, wailing like Ma Rainey for all
        those the black ox has taken away—
the little grey lady on the subway, the red Indian of the sun.
In sum, my dear externs & interns, I may be a refugee from a 3rd
        world country
recuperating in your 4th world now, but when I recover I'm off to
        the 5th!

Well, I was high as a winged-horse on astrograss & singing
        Hosannas
when they wheeled me, the sweet dove-grey Sisters of Bilitis,
down white-tiled tunnels to the house of icy waters & electric
        beds—Auschwitz for angels!
Honey, one crooned, as she strapped me in, just how many years
        do you really want?
Tapdancing between powerpoles in my metal skullcap & iron
        shoes
I heard death rattle in a baby's fist, then the juice jolted
        through me &
I'm riding the 3rd rail from Zeroville toward Ringsend—the
        Alpha Express!

Blue movie of windows brings me to a cindery river, switching
     stations, rosebrick gardens,
Sunnyside, Queens. Through cloudy curtains I see my own
     mammy, toothless, dying
in the bed I was born in. Who is that holding her in his arms?

Cap'n McCall, Sergeant Malarky, my brave night crawlers,
     wave mechanics,
after the last go-round, how will it end? Bible? Bottle? Gun?
     Breathers Anonymous?
A nanosecond of spark, then out in the dark again, in my moth-
     hole overcoat
under a starless sky? There's a chill in the air, but I know the
     way—a step at a time.
Hedgerow. Blackthorn. Elm. At the end of the lane, purple
     shadows, a faint afterglow.
Thatched roof. Plume of smoke. & the white horse standing at
     the gate, still as a stone.

from *The American Poetry Review*

JOHN ASHBERY

The Problem of Anxiety

◇ ◇ ◇

Fifty years have passed
since I started living in those dark towns
I was telling you about.
Well, not much has changed. I still can't figure out
how to get from the post office to the swings in the park.
Apple trees blossom in the cold, not from conviction,
and my hair is the color of dandelion fuzz.

Suppose this poem were about you—would *you*
put in the things I've carefully left out:
descriptions of pain, and sex, and how shiftily
people behave toward each other? Naw, that's
all in some book it seems. For you
I've saved the descriptions of finger sandwiches,
and the glass eye that stares at me in amazement
from the bronze mantel, and will never be appeased.

from *Arshile*

Camouflage

◇　◇　◇

The butterfly is the eye
of some greater creature, if we
believe the wing,
the brilliant circle which
watches and watches, waits for
its grisly chance. It's
　　　　　　　all disguise.
Or the way even sparrows
fluff and rear up
to be bigger. Bigger than
any other tiny bird,
bigger than the next day,
or the day after that
with its freezing rain,
departing berry.
　　　　　　　So the mimics come—
the starling, the mockingbird
which over and over can be anything at all:
a crow or a dove, a riff
of Mozart—scary beast—or a car door
slamming.
　　　　　　Deception *because*. Deception
since the Ice Age for some.
Secrets in the bones which aren't
whispers, in the fine
and serious brain
whose best parts
cannot think.
　　　　　　　Birds that hiss

from the nest like snakes
so the heart fails
even in a hawk.
                  And our own
big cars. Dangerous night, eyes
that blind a deer, stop it
senseless. Not an angel
wielding fire. . . .

from *Shenandoah*

No Sorry

◇   ◇   ◇

Do you have any scissors I could borrow? *No, I'm sorry I don't.* What about a knife? You got any knives? A good paring knife would do or a simple butcher knife or maybe a cleaver? *No, sorry all I have is this old bread knife my grandfather used to butter his bread with every morning.* Well then, how about a hand drill or hammer, a bike chain, or some barbed wire? You got any rusty razor-edged barbed wire? You got a chain saw? *No, sorry I don't.* Well then maybe you might have some sticks? *I'm sorry, I don't have any sticks.* How about some stones? *No, I don't have any sticks or stones.* Well how about a stone tied to a stick? *You mean a club?* Yeah, a club. You got a club? *No, sorry, I don't have any clubs.* What about some fighting picks, war axes, military forks, or tomahawks? *No, sorry, I don't have any kind of war fork, axe, or tomahawk.* What about a morning star? *A morning star?* Yeah, you know, those spiked ball and chains they sell for riot control. *No, nothing like that. Sorry.* Now, I know you said you don't have a knife except for that dull old thing your grandfather used to butter his bread with every morning and he passed down to you but I thought maybe you just might have an Australian dagger with a quartz blade and a wood handle, or a bone dagger, or a Bowie, you know it doesn't hurt to ask? Or perhaps one of those lethal multipurpose stilettos? *No, sorry.* Or maybe you have a simple blow pipe? Or a complex airgun? *No, I don't have a simple blow pipe or a complex airgun.* Well then maybe you have a jungle carbine, a Colt, a revolver, a Ruger, an axis bolt-action repeating rifle with telescopic sight for sniping, a sawed-off shotgun? Or better yet, a gas-operated self-loading fully automatic assault weapon? *No, sorry I don't.* How about a hand grenade? *No.* How about a tank? *No.* Shrapnel? *No.* Napalm? *No.* Napalm 2. *No, sorry I don't.* Let me ask you this. Do you have any intercontinental ballistic missiles? Or submarine-launched cruise missiles? Or multiple independently targeted reentry missiles? Or terminally guided anti-tank shells or projectiles? Let me ask you this. Do you have any fis-

sion bombs or hydrogen bombs? Do you have any thermonuclear war-
heads? Got any electronic measures or electronic counter-measures or
electronic counter-counter-measures? Got any biological weapons or
germ warfare, preferably in aerosol form? Got any enhanced tactical neu-
tron lasers emitting massive doses of whole-body gamma radiation? Wait
a minute. Got any plutonium? Got any chemical agents, nerve agents,
blister agents, you know, like mustard gas, any choking agents or inca-
pacitating agents or toxin agents? *Well I'm not sure. What do they look like?*
Liquid vapor powder colorless gas. Invisible. *I'm not sure. What do they smell
like?* They smell like fruit, garlic, fish or soap, new-mown hay, apple blos-
soms, or like those little green peppers that your grandfather probably
would tend to in his garden every morning after he buttered his bread
with that old bread knife that he passed down to you.

from *TriQuarterly*

Love Song

◊ ◊ ◊

If you were drowning, I'd come to the rescue,
    wrap you in my blanket and pour hot tea.
If I were a sheriff, I'd arrest you
    and keep you in the cell under lock and key.

If you were a bird, I'd cut a record
    and listen all night long to your high-pitched trill.
If I were a sergeant, you'd be my recruit,
    and boy I can assure you you'd love the drill.

If you were Chinese, I'd learn the language,
    burn a lot of incense, wear funny clothes.
If you were a mirror, I'd storm the Ladies,
    give you my red lipstick and puff your nose.

If you loved volcanoes, I'd be lava
    relentlessly erupting from my hidden source.
And if you were my wife, I'd be your lover
    because the church is firmly against divorce.

from *The New Republic*

Feminine Intuition

◇ ◇ ◇

I. LITTLE RED RIDING HOOD

Astrid comes from upstate New York.
She comes from distress.
She's enthusiastic about it.
She doesn't belong, but she tries hard.
Her husband hurts her, but they have a drug-free life.
They roller skate and take up fads enthusiastically,
Neon clothing and the like.
He's an air traffic controller, so they move constantly.
This time it's California. After the picnic
I said, "She reminds me of Little Red Riding Hood."
My husband said, "Yeah."
We were doing the dishes.
I can't say some other things, so I say this.

II. PLASTIC SURGERY, SKIPPED DESSERT

That simple woman thought I was simple, but I was not.
I was never simple.
Not trees, stars, plot.
She smoked her fingers down to the yellow.
She had the harsh hearty laughter
Of the women who believe the men will leave them.
All the mothers I knew went nuts.
Hair the color of a screwdriver.
It's a cliché, but it's an altar.
Cotton candy spun into a knot.

47

Especially rich women, with art.
Kimono, muumuu.
Ice cubes.

But I was never simple. I was never simple.
The way I was raised, the men never leave a woman.
She was a woman: I could not trust her.

III. A WOMAN CLOTHED WITH THE SUN

Imagine, all over America, women are losing bone mass.

Brittle old ladies: we create them.
Coiffured movie sirens lounging around the pool transmogrify
into brittle old sea hags.
(They don't know anything: they just nag.)
Let's let them swim out to sea.
Let's give them a spiny seahorse to ride on.
"Goodbye brittle old ladies, beautiful ones—
Ride out against the horizon and the orange sun!"

from *The American Poetry Review*

The Map Room

◇ ◇ ◇

We moved into a house with 6 rooms: the Bedroom,
the Map Room, the Vegas Room, Cities
in the Flood Plains, the West, & the Room Which Contains All
of Mexico. We honeymooned in the Vegas Room where
lounge acts wasted our precious time. Then there was the junta's
high command, sick dogs of the Map Room, heel-
prints everywhere, pushing model armies into the unfurnished
West. At night: stories of their abandoned homes in the Cities
in the Flood Plains, how they had loved each other
mercilessly, in rusting cars, until the drive-in went under.
From the Bedroom we called the decorator & demanded
a figurehead . . . the one true diva to be had
in All of Mexico: Maria Felix [star of *The Devourer,* star
of *The Lady General*]. Nightly in Vegas, "It's Not Unusual"
or the Sex Pistols medley. Nothing ever comes back
from the West, it's a one-way door, a one-shot deal,—
the one room we never slept in together. My wife
wants to rename it The Ugly Truth. I love my wife for her
wonderful, light, creamy, highly reflective skin;
if there's an illumination from the submerged Cities,
that's her. She suspects me of certain acts involving Maria Felix,
the gambling debts mount . . . but when she sends the junta off to
        Bed
we rendezvous in the Map Room & sprawl across the New World
with our heads to the West. I sing her romantic melodies from the
        Room
Which Contains All of Mexico, tunes which keep arriving
like heaven, in waves of raw data, & though I wrote

none of the songs myself & can't pronounce them, these are my
greatest hits

from The Iowa Review

Lines Lost Among Trees

◇　◇　◇

These are not the lines that came to me
while walking in the woods
with no pen
and nothing to write on anyway.

They are gone forever,
a handful of coins
dropped through the grate of memory,
along with the ingenious mnemonic

I devised to hold them in place—
all gone and forgotten
before I had returned to the clearing of lawn
in back of our quiet house

with its jars jammed with pens,
its notebooks and reams of blank paper,
its desk and soft lamp,
its table and the light from its windows.

So this is my elegy for them,
those six or eight exhalations,
the braided rope of the syntax,
the jazz of the timing,

and the little insight at the end
wagging like the short tail
of a perfectly obedient spaniel
sitting by the door.

This is my envoy to nothing
where I say Go, little poem—
not out into the world of strangers' eyes,
but off to some airy limbo,

home to lost epics,
unremembered names,
and fugitive dreams
such as the one I had last night,

which, like a fantastic city in pencil,
erased itself
in the bright morning air
just as I was waking up.

from *Poetry*

The Sky Drank In

◊　◊　◊

The sky drank in sparrows making lucid the oaks.
The shadow dropped beneath the stair.

And you as you were,
I as I become,

color and form, wake and start, split one
on the other side of the screen of your projections—

you wanted me.
But I wasn't around,

only a small soul asleep in the high heel,
or fluttering among the cosmetics

blindly, usually just a pause
between what's there and not there,

mail on the stoop,
lists "to do"

and other narcotics we call beauty, symmetry, harmony,
and no interior thing—

　　　　Only a weak-edged soul,
the almost seen luminous circle breaking

to parenthesis, tender embrace trying to enclose
whether for an instant or an eternity, something is "true—"

In the time that is welcome,
time that does not take away,

whirl of particles in the desire of whatever I sought
when I began these sentences

                                    (I stay, I have stayed, I am staying)

the slow burning off of self exhausts us,
the come on darling, the salesman, the waitress,

the couple fighting in the phone booth
heart wall to heart wall,

palm, darkening lip, the infinities that *were, were*
our mouths and our sex—

That which was lost becoming lost again—

lovers in the used world,

                        more extinguished, finer,

o you-again,

        o one, o no one, o you—

        from *American Letters & Commentary*

The Heavy Headed Dance

◇ ◇ ◇

for Mel & Ted

I am dancing &
on my head
is the spotted skunk
whose scent did not protect it
from Mr. & Mrs. Archibald of Texas

On my head
is the stuffed bobcat
whose facial expression was set
by the taxidermy department

On my head
is a bull caught
in the act of masturbation
& on top of that
rides the moose
stunned-gunned while wading in a lake
& on top of that
are the monkeys
entrapped while urinating
& on top of that
lay the hyena
jackal & vulture
shot while eating from zebra carcasses
& on top of that
sits the ram with

largest horn on record
donated by Henry Beck

& with all the stuffed animals piled on my head
I am dancing past
lyricist with the baboon heart

I am dancing like a dog
in front of financial consultant
implanted with pig genes

I am dancing & fluttering like a butterfly
across from the novelist posing
in a beaver skin coat

I am dancing near the astronomer
who circles the floor with her
uplifted face frozen like a tiger

I am dancing against window
of artificial coyotes
& howling with contemporary African band
in the grizzly bear room

I am dancing my pangolin hairdo dance
past the river of ants in panties
of gyrating vocal groups

I am dancing so many different dances
with so many bloated animals
dead on my head
that my head is
a dancing museum of unnatural history
& I am dancing where I cannot see
myself dancing
to know why I am dancing
but I am dancing
I am dancing

from *Hanging Loose*

Won't It Be Fine?

◊ ◊ ◊

At whatever age he was, he was apt with that
"not with a bang but a whimper . . ." Wiseass little
prick felt himself thus projected an impervious
balloon into history. Or maybe not at all so,

just spooked he had blown it again or been blown
out by old-time time's indifference to anything
wouldn't fit the so-called pattern. I am tired, I am
increasingly crippled by my own body's real wear

and tear, and lend my mind to an obsessional search for
les images des jeunes filles or again not so
young at all with huge tits, or come-hither looks,
or whatever my failing head now projects as desirable.

What was I looking at sunk once full weight onto others,
some of whom I hardly knew or even wanted to, mean-
minded bastard that I was and must perforce continue
to be. God help us all who have such fathers, or lovers,

as I feel myself to have been, be, and think to spend
quiet evenings at home while he (me), or they, plural,
pad the feral passages, still in their bedroom slippers,
never dressing anymore but peering out, distracted,

for the mailman, the fellow with the packages, the persons
having the wrong address, or even an unexpected friend appearing.
"No, I never go out anymore, having all I need right here"—
and looks at his wife, children, the dog, as if they were only

a defense. Because where he has been and is cannot admit them. He has made a tediously contrived "thing to do today" with his own thing, short of cutting it off. There is no hope in hope, friends. If you have friends, be sure you are good to them.

from *Grand Street*

History

◇ ◇ ◇

I too could give my heart to history.
I too could turn to it for illumination,
For a definition of who we are, what it means to live here
Breathing this atmosphere at the end of the century.
I too could agree we aren't pilgrims
Resting for the night at a roadside hermitage,
Uncertain about the local language and customs,
But more like the bushes and trees around us
Sprung from this soil, nurtured by the annual rainfall
And the slant of the sun in our temperate latitudes.

If only history didn't side with survivors,
The puny ones who in times of famine
Can live on nothing, or the big and greedy.
If only it didn't conclude that the rebels who take the fort
Must carry the flag of the future in their knapsacks,
While the rebels who fail have confused their babel
With the voice of the people, which announces by instinct
The one and only path to posterity.

The people are far away in the provinces
With their feet on the coffee table
Leafing through magazines on barbecuing and sailing.
They're dressing to go to an uncle's funeral,
To a daughter's rehearsal dinner. They're listening,
As they drive to work, to the radio.
Caesar's ad on law and order seems thoughtful.
Brutus's makes some useful points about tyranny.
But is either candidate likely to keep his promises?

When ice floes smashed the barges on the Delaware
And Washington drowned with all his men, it was clear
To the world the revolt he led against excise taxes
And import duties was an over-reaction.
When the South routed the North at Gettysburg,
It was clear the scheme of merchants to impose their values
On cotton planters was doomed from the start
Along with Lincoln's mystical notion of union,
Which sadly confused the time-bound world we live in
With a world where credos don't wear out.

from *The New Republic*

The Death of John Berryman

◇ ◇ ◇

Henry went over the edge of the bridge first; he always did.
Then Mr. Interlocutor and Mr. Bones, then the blackface minstrels
with their tambourines. You have to empty out
all of the contents before the person himself dies.

The beard went over the edge, and Stephen Crane,
and the never-completed scholarly work on Shakespeare,
and faculty wives, and a sheaf of recovery wards
white-tiled in the blue shadow of the little hours.

He loosened his necktie and the recurrent dream
of walking out under water to the destined island.
His mother went over in pearls; his father went over.
His real father went over, whoever his father was.

He thought to go over with someone, hand in hand
with perhaps Mistress Bradstreet, but someone always preceded him.
The news of his death preceded him. It hit the water
with a fat splash and the target twanged.

When there was nothing to see with or hear with, the silent traffic
of bystanders wrapped in snow, his only body
let itself loose, turned and waved before it went over
to what it could never understand as being the human shore.

from *Poetry*

How Should I Say This?

◇ ◇ ◇

Should I say the eyes were laced and that the laces were snakes
that crawled through these eyes.
Should I say that the mouth was hollow and green,
that the tongue was crossed and tied,
that the canvas was stretched and salt-stained,
that the blood was bleached, that the sole was split,
that the holes were hard-packed with red clay.
Should I say that the leather was cracked and bone-white,
that the boot was tagged, that the foot itself was big.
Should I say that this was all of the world
and none of the world to me. Should I say that the bags leaked
sand and the sand formed a cone-shaped mound beside the boot.
Should I say the sand told no time, that the watch was changing,
that the bunkers were abandoned and the big guns unmanned.
Should I say that. Should I say the sun was ice-white
or should I say it was running or withdrawn or should I just forget
the way it passed over the bold blue body
that was a color you'll never know.
Should I say that a new hot rain was beginning
to fall at the end of one more blocked out day.
Should I say that someone rifled through his gear.
Should I say that someone in a hooch was drunk,
that someone was playing Gershwin,
that someone else fired up a number
and passed it on hand to hand, mouth to mouth.
Should I say that nobody was in support,
that no steps were taken.
Should I say that the flags were draped.
Or should I say the flags hung limp as coats on hooks.

Should I say what it was you did. Go on. Say it.
Say you doused the drums with diesel.
I doused the drums with diesel. I started the fires
to burn our stacked waste. No, say this instead, say our stacked shit.
And say this, don't save it, say the oily smoke curled
into ribbons and that the ribbons rose into the sunlit rain.
Say no, I did not think, not of home, not of mother, not of you.
Say you hid. I always hid. Say you were remote.
Say you were mute.
Say your eyes are speaking now.
Say you retreated into the sleeve of your fatigue
and sucked salt and that you shifted your eyes
from the flaming drums
to the boot still standing out on the sun-scorched earth this day.

from *Massachusetts Review*

Atomic Bride

◇ ◇ ◇

For Andre Foxxe

A good show
Starts in the
Dressing room

And works its way
To the stage.
Close the door,

Andre's cross-
dressing, what
A drag. All

The world loves
A bride, something
About those gowns.

A good wedding
Starts in the
Department store

And works its way
Into the photo album.
Close the door,

Andre's tying
The knot, what
A drag. Isn't he

Lovely? All
The world loves
A bachelor, some-

thing about glamour
& glitz, white
Shirts, lawsuits.

A good dog
Starts in the yard
And works its way

Into da house.
Close your eyes,
Andre's wide open.

One freak of the week
Per night, what
A drag. Isn't

He lovely? All
The world loves
A nuclear family,

Something about
A suburban home,
Chaos in order.

A good bride starts
In the laboratory
And works his way

To the church.
Close the door,
Andre's thinking

Things over, what
A drag. Isn't
He lovely? All

The world loves
A divorce, something
About broken vows.

A good war starts
In the courtroom
And works its way

To the album cover.
Close the door,
Andre's swearing in,

What a drag.
Isn't he lovely? All
The world loves

A star witness,
Something about
Cross-examination.

A good drug starts
In Washington
And works its way

To the dancefloor.
Close the door,
Andre's strungout,

What a drag,
Isn't he lovely? All
The world loves

Rhythm guitar,
Something about
Those warm chords.

A good skeleton
Starts in the closet
And works its way

To the top of the charts.
Start the organ.
Andre's on his way

Down the aisle,
Alone, what an encore. All
The world loves

An explosive ending.
Go ahead Andre,
Toss the bouquet.

from *Ploughshares*

You Know
What I'm Saying?

◊ ◊ ◊

"I favor your enterprise," the soup ladle says.
"And I regard you and your project with joy."

At Grand Forks where the road divides twice over,
the wet wooden squeegee handle poking out
of the bucket beside the red gas pump tells you,
"*Whichever* way—hey, for you they're *all* okay."

The stunted pine declares from someone's backyard
you happen to be passing, "I don't begrudge you
your good health. In fact, my blessing—you've got it, now."

An ironing board is irrepressible.
"Your success is far from certain, my friend,
and still it's vital to my happiness."

The yellow kernels in the dust, mere chickenfeed,
call out, "We salute you, and you can count on us."

We do not live in a world of things
but among benedictions given
and—do you know what I'm saying?—received.

from *Poetry*

Asylum

◇   ◇   ◇

For Jessica

My life becomes too hard, so I go away.
A couple near Turlock takes me in,
not because they like me,

but they like the good my rent will do.
It's just the two and the woman's mother,
frail and shawled in black.

As spring heats into summer,
the old woman comes to call me "son,"
for we have both lost sense of home.

At meals they barely feed her,
give her the smallest cuts of meat,
mostly fat, and a few red drops of wine.

They do not speak.
She convinces me they want to kill her—
"Neglect is only the beginning."

One afternoon, outside their farmhouse,
we sit on crates and smell yams
swelling in the warm earth.

I ask her why she lives like this,
but she says nothing, only smiles,
grabs a chicken, and wrings its neck,

then pulls out its innards,
showing me the freshly eaten grain
inside the dark gizzard.

She frowns at my silence, as if to say,
"There is a lesson here,
but you do not understand it yet."

Later, as the moon begins its nightly rounds,
she leads me a little ways from town,
to a tree clutching a fallen ax's rusting blade.

She says it was the *tree* that bit,
catching the ax head
and snapping the handle in two.

Come autumn,
she offers me the ax that lost its head,
and I go south to face my life.

from *The Gettysburg Review*

Backing into the Future

◇ ◇ ◇

Little hints of reality march across the back
Of the bus I'm not riding on as it disappears
Into the sunlight registered on my eyeballs.
A quarantine falls over the picture
And it is like nothing was ever there
Or rather there seems to be a bug there
On the slide I am examining that doesn't figure
Because I need a drink and I don't drink.

There must be some horrible reason
Why I'm here in this stainless steel capsule
With a note in my hand addressed to the people
Of the 23rd Century. It's like the doors
Suddenly fret open & I am deep underground
With Ted Berrigan and we both have an intense
Distrust of the future we are looking forward to

And then a dog walks through a window
So I flick it back into my subconscious
A sort of canine flashlight I can use
To discover the lay of the land,
Pastures of my childhood that no one seemed
Interested in neglecting, all mine to assume,
Bright quadrangles opening on a square
I knew was me

from *The World*

Introductions

◊ ◊ ◊

I remember the miniature and plastic saints
of childhood better than the names of men I met
in the maybe war and I remember those better than
my children's friends and I remember them
better than the man I talked to last week on the telephone
who may buy five thousand pairs of the underwear I have
to sell to meet my quota this month or else.

And I have to meet that man tonight, among people
that I do know and do remember and he doesn't
and I have to introduce him as if I knew his name
as well as I know my brother's, who I sometimes
can hardly remember at all anymore, he having left home with
all the toys and half our parents' lives before I had a chance
to tell him goodbye and went off and didn't remember one night
(so I have heard, so the story goes, so I tell my kids)
to put his flak jacket on before he went out to take a piss
and instead took a bullet through his stomach that took
one week's worth of pain to realize he was never going to digest
and died and I remember better even than my children's names
the day we got his mess kit back from the US ARMY, courtesy
of the RED CROSS of America, and inside it was tucked this three
inch plastic Blessed Virgin Mary, the same one that one of us,
I can't remember which, got as a prize for selling the most
punch-out card chances for some gigantic gift that I forget
but probably had to do with a Chocolate Easter Bunny
stuffed with jelly beans or a subscription to *Boy's Life,*
or *The Messenger of the Sacred Heart.*

So tonight, when it's all on the line, when I am about
to be hung out to dry like those 5,000 jockey shorts I will
never sell after this insult, I'll lean back on the air
as if my brother were there holding me up, I'll reach
inside my watch pocket of the vest I only wear
when it's all on the line and fondle for luck the 3-inch
plastic BVM that I have kept for more years
than I can remember and then I will remember
the fool's name just like that. Or else, like that, I won't.

from *Poetry*

A Fan Letter

◇ ◇ ◇

Dear Literary Hero,

Now that you've gently
slit open my envelope,
you see naked before you
on this plain drugstore stationery
watermarked with my tears,
the shaky handwriting of one
who has been given a second chance
and desires to use it wisely.
Allow me to tell you a little
about myself. Before I was wiped
clean as the gilt-edged mirror
in my favorite gas station
lavatory—in other words,
prior to being remade
into a reflective, immaculate being
by ingesting physician-approved
chemicals, potent as the emollients
in lemon-scented furniture polish—
I felt compelled to sleep
with a grim local widower's
limp twin sons. Then I digressed
to the widower. Still unsatisfied,
I found myself eyeing
his shaggy Scottish deerhounds,
at which point I thought it best
to leave town quietly, by midnight bus,
and take up residence where

I wouldn't continue to shame
my prominent family, dashing
their political ambitions.
Brimming with remorse,
I legally changed my name
and that same night tried
to end my life in bungalow 444
of a cheap roadside motel
called The Log Cabin,
by consuming fool's parsley,
a fungus containing
several toxic compounds.
I didn't even get high.
Dread left a taste in my mouth
like old-fashioned cough syrup
flavored with horehound.
One of my cheeks
went perpetually red.
The other remained deathly pale.
I began to hang around
with old beer drinkers, to want
to lie down all the time.
I noticed a bubbling sensation
around my navel, which emitted
a squeaky hiss, as though
I were a punctured tire
leaking air. It became apparent
my poor tongue, which looked
like a dried orange peel,
was suddenly eight or nine inches
too long, an infirmity
which interfered with wound-licking
and wallpaper-tasting.
Yours truly was in a bad way!
I craved meals of charcoal
and discarded tea bags, but consoled
myself with the contents
of coffee shop ashtrays. Doors
became my nemesis—I had to
unhinge them or become unhinged

myself. Then, in the hospital,
one of the meanest ward nurses
had your recent book sticking out
of her huge, shabby purse.
I filched it, just to get
under her skin. Was I surprised,
upon opening your tome and perusing
the first paragraph, to realize
my dark days were almost over.
These pages contained my salvation.
I read and recovered. Your sentences
gave me the kick in the teeth I
sorely needed. The voice of your thoughts
woke me like a rooster announcing
the end of the world, or maybe
a raven who'd grown teeth and learned
to warble bawdy songs. Your seething words
cured me—reading each was like swallowing
leaf after leaf of a blessed, healing salad
made from ambrosia and ragweed.
I think we should meet. Every night
I stare at the photo of you
on your book's back flap, sitting
in a brocade overstuffed armchair,
smoking your pipe that resembles
a boar's tusk. I close my eyes
and perceive myself curled up
so cozily in your lap, and after that
I see the bright mayhem
of millions of fireworks,
lighting up the dark sky
of our like minds.

from *The American Poetry Review*

Is About

◊   ◊   ◊

Dylan is about the Individual against the whole of creation
Beethoven is about one man's fist in the lightning clouds
The Pope is about abortion & the spirits of the dead . . .
Television is about people sitting in their living room looking at
    their things
America is about being a big Country full of Cowboys Indians Jews
    Negroes & Americans
Orientals Chicanos Factories skyscrapers Niagara Falls Steel Mills
    radios homeless Conservatives, don't forget
Russia is about Czars Stalin Poetry Secret Police Communism
    barefoot in the snow
But that's not really Russia it's a concept
A concept is about how to look at the earth from the moon
without ever getting there. The moon is about love & Werewolves,
    also Poe.
Poe is about looking at the moon from the sun
or else the graveyard
Everything is about something if you're a thin movie producer
    chain-smoking muggles
The world is about overpopulation, Imperial invasions, Biocide,
    Genocide, Fratricidal Wars, Starvation, Holocaust, mass injury &
        murder, high technology
Super science, atom Nuclear Neutron Hydrogen detritus, Radiation
    Compassion Buddha, Alchemy
Communication is about monopoly television radio movie newspaper
    spin on Earth, i.e. planetary censorship.
Universe is about Universe.
Allen Ginsberg is about confused mind writing down newspaper
    headlines from Mars—

The audience is about salvation, the listeners are about sex,
    Spiritual gymnastics, nostalgia for the Steam Engine & Pony
    Express
Hitler Stalin Roosevelt & Churchill are about arithmetic &
    Quadrilateral equations, above all chemistry physics & chaos
    theory—
Who cares what it's all about?
I do! Edgar Allan Poe cares! Shelley cares! Beethoven & Dylan care.
Do you care? What are you about
or are you a human being with 10 fingers & two eyes?

New York City October 24, 1995

from *The New Yorker*

DANA GIOIA

The Litany

◇　◇　◇

This is a litany of lost things,
a canon of possessions dispossessed,
a photograph, an old address, a key.
It is a list of words to memorize
or to forget—of *amo, amas, amat,*
the conjugations of a dead tongue
in which the final sentence has been spoken.

This is the liturgy of rain,
falling on mountain, field, and ocean—
indifferent, anonymous, complete—
of water infinitesimally slow,
sifting through rock, pooling in darkness,
gathering in springs, then rising without our agency,
only to dissolve in mist or cloud or dew.

This is a prayer to unbelief,
to candles guttering and darkness undivided,
to incense drifting into emptiness.
It is the smile of a stone madonna
and the solar fury of the consecrated wine,
a benediction on the death of a young god,
brave and beautiful, rotting on a tree.

This is a litany to earth and ashes,
to the dust of roads and vacant rooms,
to the fine silt circling in a shaft of sun,
settling indifferently on books and beds.
This is a prayer to praise what we become,

"Dust thou art, to dust thou shalt return."
Savor its taste—the bitterness of earth and ashes.

This is a prayer, inchoate and unfinished,
for you, my love, my loss, my lesion,
a rosary of words to count out time's
illusions, all the minutes, hours, days
the calendar compounds as if the past
existed somewhat—like an inheritance
still waiting to be claimed.

Until at last it is our litany, *mon vieux,*
my reader, my voyeur, as if the mist
steaming from the gorge, this pure paradox,
the shattered river rising as it falls—
splintering the light, swirling it skyward,
neither transparent nor opaque but luminous,
even as it vanishes—were not our life.

from *The Hudson Review*

Smoking

◇   ◇   ◇

I like the cool and heft of it, dull metal on the palm,
And the click, the hiss, the spark fuming into flame,
Boldface of fire, the rage and sway of it, raw blue at the base
And a slope of gold, a touch to the packed tobacco, the tip
Turned red as a warning light, blown brighter by the breath,
The pull and the pump of it, and the paper's white
Smoothed now to ash as the smoke draws back, drawn down
To the black crust of lungs, tar and poisons in the pink,
And the blood sorting it out, veins tight and the heart slow,
The push and wheeze of it, a sweep of plumes in the air
Like a shako of horses dragging a hearse through the late centennium,
London, at the end of December, in the dark and fog.

from *Shenandoah*

KATE GLEASON

After Fighting for Hours

◊   ◊   ◊

When all else fails
we fall to making love,
our bodies like the pioneers
in rough covered wagons
whose oxen strained to cross the Rockies
until their hearts gave out trying,
those pioneers who had out-survived
fever, hunger, a run of broken luck,
those able-bodied men and women
who simply unlocked the animals
from their yokes, and taking
the hitches in their own hands, pulled
by the sheer desire of their bodies
their earthly goods over the divide.

from *Green Mountains Review*

ALBERT GOLDBARTH

Complete with Starry Night
and Bourbon Shots

◇ ◇ ◇

Morgan's father will be mailed to her,
they've said in a letter—now that every bequested
dole of his body has been banked away,
the residue in its factory urn will be mailed.
She says Stephanie sometimes wiggles her fingers around
inside *her* father, so the bone chips
clink against the fired clay, and I suggest
the final char of Bob Potts be sealed inside maracas;
"He'd like that," Morgan says, especially if the Texas
Sexoramas used him percussively, his favorite
country-funk group. What she'll really do
this June is scatter him into the air
of Mt. Palomar "because he loved his telescope." Let him
circle and settle, circle, circle and settle.

★ ★ ★

He also loved his drink, but no one mentions
touring the Pearl Beer plant and surreptitiously adding him
to a vat. The stories are legion,
legend: for instance Bill English of English's Bar
in one clean squeeze deadeyeing a shotglass
off his pate. Though now that's decades gone.
When I met him even his *teeth* were grizzled
—up at the bar surrounded by all of the gleaming
palomino hotpants 20-year-olds of Austin, Texas;

reading Kipling's *Kim* in the sonic boomboom rock.
I first ate pit-cooked cabrito at one of his parties,
lank and sharp and good. Then doing our names
on the lawn, from the bones—in the light,
and in the easiness, before anything like that seemed symbolic.

★ ★ ★

The Wild West–style saloon doors of "The Hall of Horns"
(the Brewery's tourist annex) open grandly on its choice, thematic
gawkables: a map of the United States entirely
done from snake rattles; sturdy desks, and chairs, and armoires
completely or near-completely from antlers and hooves.
Also the monstrosities: the siamese twin calves
with braided horns, like a Swedish Christmas candle;
the calf with horns that horribly loop forward and enter
its eyesockets. Yes, and there were those Victorian museums
of human residue: the brains of criminals floating like compote,
the gold-cased tibia and jaws of saints. Our wonderment
can seize on something commoner than these, without
diminishing: a skeleton of an owl, and the ribs of its digested
fieldmouse suddenly tumbling out.

★ ★ ★

Because he loved his telescope . . . he's being flung under
everything above, the whole night sky is called upon
to be his memorial marker. Maybe our obligation
is finding lines from star to star up there:
the new bones of his new, if metaphysical,
existence. Etc. etc.—sky and bones, the stuff
of sonnets. Some people like calling the heavens
star-complected, to some that's "precious" odium. Tastes
differ. My father was heavily lowered into the earth,
is earth by now, is the dry click of ants in the grasses.
Still, I think that they might meet at the horizonline,
Bob Potts and my father. Maybe they're having a metaphysical
quaff right now, remembering how one's son and one's daughter
divorced each other—one of the copious little deaths.

★ ★ ★

Even microscopic radiolarians have skeletons, and this
alone can jolt our cogitation meters into the red
astonishment zone—what then to make of Morgan's parcel
flying through the mails? Not that comedy, say, or bereavement
are matters of size. And still it's the whale I think of,
washed ashore in 1564 on Nod Thwaite's property:
yes, the whale would do, as a unit for Morgan to measure by.
Thwaite cleaned each stave, and on a brisking autumn day
when his buffing was done, began to charge admission to that osseous
parthenon. Hundreds took the tour. By night a fire
threw the vaulting into flickery relief. By day they clambered
their midget way among these ruins. I like them mostly
in the skull; as if a whale were dreaming of what it had been
before it turned from that and chose the sea.

★ ★ ★

I'm sorry, but this gray vase bearing gray debris,
this poof and its stringbean pieces of bone, is no
Bob Potts in his cardigan flecked with pipe shag
holding court at The Cedar Door or Mulligan's.
No. This vase is Nothing; its contents, Nothing.
And Nothing can't be counterbalanced. I'm sorry,
there isn't a fact that can do it, there isn't
a richly glitzed-up fiction in the world, not God,
not no-God, there isn't a memory that means anything
to Nothing. And Morgan says, with a tender shake of her head,
"That man," as if he might have been some feathercrested
platinum-shitting prodigy, "was something."
Even without his eyes he was something, without
his legs, and in the final sour bubble of breathing: something.

★ ★ ★

Because he loved his telescope . . . he's given away
to that emptiness now, he's sprinkled from a daughter's fingers
into the galaxy pinch by pinch. As physics knows,
and so as endless poems these days repeat, we're all
constructed of the particles of stars. The service

may as well go *dust to dust, and astra to astra.*
Not that any rhetoric really comforts.
Not that any glint of wit or thundered scripture
suffices for long. But since you've asked for a poem,
my ex, my sweet and troubled one, I'll give you this
attempt, complete with starry night and bourbon shots:
Here,
I'm lifting a beer
for Bob Potts.

                    from *Quarterly West*

Thinking

◇   ◇   ◇

I can't really remember now. The soundless foamed.
A crow clung like a cough to a wire above me. There was a chill.
It was a version of a crow, untitled as such, tightly feathered
in the chafing air. Rain was expected. All round him air
dilated, as if my steady glance on him, cindering at the glance-core where
it held him tightest, swelled and sucked,
while round that core, first a transition, granular—then remembrance of
                                                    thing being
seen—remembrance as it thins-out into matter, almost listless—then,
sorrow—if sorrow could be sterile—and the rest fraying off into all the
                                                    directions,
variegated amnesias—lawns, black panes, screens the daylight
thralls into in search of well-edged things. . . . If I squint, he glints.
The wire he's on wobbly and his grip not firm.
Lifting each forked clawgrip again and again.
Every bit of wind toying with his hive of black balance.
Every now and then a passing car underneath causing a quick rearrange-
                                                    ment.
The phonelines from six houses, and the powerlines from three
grouped-up above me, some first-rung of sky, him not comfortable,
nature silted-in to this maximum habitat—*freedom*—
passers-by (woman and dog) vaguely relevant I'd guess though he doesn't
                                                    look down,
eyeing all round, disqualifying, disqualifying
all the bits within radius that hold no clue
of whatever is sought, urgent but without hurry,
me still by this hedge now, waiting for his black to blossom,
then wing-thrash where he falls at first against the powerline,
then updraft seized, gravity winnowed, the falling raggedly

reversed, depth suddenly pursued, its invisibility ridged—bless him—
until he is off, hinge by hinge, built of tiny wingtucks, filaments
of flapped-back wind, until the thing (along whose spine
his sentence of black talk, thrashing, wrinkling, dissipates—the history,
                                                    the wiring,
shaking, with light—) is born.

from *The New Republic*

DONALD HALL

The Porcelain Couple

◊   ◊   ◊

When Jane felt well enough for me to leave her
for a whole day, I drove south by the river
to empty my mother Lucy's house in Connecticut.
I hurried from room to room, cellar to attic,
opening a crammed closet, then turning
to discover a chest with five full drawers.
I labelled for shipping sofas and chairs,
bedroom sets, and tables; I wrapped figurines
and fancy teacups in paper, preserving things
she cherished—and dreaded, in her last years,
might go for a nickel on the Spring Glen lawn.
Everywhere I looked I saw shelves and tabletops
covered with Lucy's glass animals and music boxes.
Everywhere in closets, decades of dresses hung
in dead air. I carried garbage bags in one hand,
and with the other swept my mother's leftover
possessions into sacks for the Hamden dump.
I stuffed bags full of blouses, handkerchiefs,
and the green-gold dress she wore to Bermuda.
At the last moment I discovered and saved
a cut-glass tumbler, stained red at the top,
Lucy 1905 scripted on the stain. In the garage
I piled the clanking bags, then drove four hours
north with my hands tight on the Honda's wheel,
drank a beer looking through Saturday's mail,
pitched into bed beside Jane fitfully asleep,
and woke exhausted from rolling unendable
nightmares of traffic and fire. In my dreams
I grieved or mourned interchangeably for Lucy,

for Lucy's things, for Jane, and for me.
When I woke, I rose as if from a drunken sleep
after looting a city and burning its temples.
All day as I ate lunch or counted out pills,
or as we lay weeping, hugging in bed together,
I counted precious things from our twenty years:
a blue vase, a candelabrum Jane carried on her lap
from the Baja, and the small porcelain box
from France I found under the tree one Christmas
where a couple in relief stretch out asleep,
like a catafalque, on the pastel double bed
of the box's top, both wearing pretty nightcaps.

from *The New Yorker*

Her Body

◇   ◇   ◇

1. THE FINGERS

They are small enough to find and care for a tiny stone.
  To lift it with wobbly concentration from the ground,
    from the family of stones, up past the pursed mouth—

for this we are thankful—to a place level with her eyes
  to take a close look, a look into the nature of stone.
    Like everything, it is for the first time: first stone,

chilly cube of ice, soft rise of warm flesh, hard
  surface of table leg, first and lasting scent of grass
    rubbed between the tiny pincer fingers. And there is

the smallest finger poking the air, pointing toward the first heat
  of the single sun, pointing toward the friendly angels
    who sent her, letting them know contact's made.

2. THE EYES

We believe their color makes some kind of difference,
the cast of it played off the color of hair and face.

But it makes no difference, blue or brown,
hazel, green, or gray, pale sky or sand.

When sleep-burdened they'll turn up into her,
close back down upon her sizeable will.

But when she's ready for the yet-to-come—
oh, they widen, grow a deep cool sheen

to catch the available light and shine
with the intensity of the newly arrived.

If they find you they'll hold on relentlessly
without guile, the gaze no less than interrogatory,

fixed, immediate, bringing to bear what there's been
to date. Call her name and perhaps they'll turn to you,

or they might be engaged, looking deeply into the nature
of other things—the affect of wall, the texture of rug,

into something very small that's fallen to the floor
and needs to be isolated and controlled. Maybe

an afternoon reflection, an insect moving *slowly,*
maybe just looking with loyalty into the eyes of another.

3. The Toes

Who went to market?
Who stayed home?
This one goes,
this one doesn't.
This one eats

the flesh
of grass-eating mammals,
this one does not.
In the seventeenth century
Basho—delicate master

of the vagaries of who
went where—
wrote to one he loved

not of market
and not of meat,

but something brief,
abbreviated,
like five unburdened toes
fluttering like cilia
in the joy of a drafty room:

> *You go,*
> *I stay.*
> *Two autumns.*

4. THE SOUL

Who knows how they get here,
beyond the obvious.
Who packaged the code

that provided the slate for her eyes,
and what about the workmanship
that went into the fingers

allowing such intricate movement
just months from the other side?—
Who placed with such exactness

the minute nails on each
of the ten unpainted toes?
And what remains

beyond eye and ear, the thing
most deeply rooted in her body—
the thing that endlessly blossoms

but doesn't age, in time
shows greater vitality? The thing
unlike the body that so quickly

reaches its highest moment only
to begin, with little hesitation,
the long roll back, slowing all the way

until movement is administered
by devices other than those devised
by divine design? The ageless thing

we call *soul,* like air, both resident
and owner of the body's estate.
But *her* soul, only partially

unpackaged, sings
through the slate that guards it,
contacts those of us waiting here

with a splay of its soft,
scrutinizing fingers.
Her soul is a sapling thing,

something green, dew-damp
but resolute, entering this world
with an angel's thumb pressed

to her unformed body at the very last,
a template affixed to her body
when they decided it was time

to let her go, for her to come to us
and their good work was done.
An angel's thumbprint, a signature, her soul.

from *Ploughshares*

Interrupted Meditation

◇ ◇ ◇

Little green involute fronds of fern at creekside.
And the sinewy clear water rushing over creekstone
of the palest amber, veined with a darker gold,
thinnest lines of gold rivering through the amber
like—ah, now we come to it. *We were not put on earth,*
the old man said, he was hacking into the crust
of a sourdough half loaf in his vehement, impatient way
with an old horn-handled knife, *to express ourselves.*
I knew he had seen whole cities leveled. Also
that there had been a time of shame for him, outskirts
of a ruined town, half Baroque, half Greek Revival,
pediments of Flora and Hygeia from a brief eighteenth century
health spa boom lying on the streets in broken chunks
and dogs scavenging among them. His one act of courage
then had been to drop pieces of bread or chocolate,
as others did, where a fugitive family of Jews
was rumored to be hiding. *I never raised my voice,*
of course, none of us did. He sliced wedges of cheese
after the bread, spooned out dollops of sour jam
from some Hungarian plum, purple and faintly gingered.
Every day the bits of half-mildewed, dry, hard—
this is my invention—whitened chocolate, dropped furtively
into rubble by the abandoned outbuilding of some suburban
mechanic's shop—but I am sure he said chocolate—
and it comforted no one. *We talked in whispers.*
"Someone is taking them." "Yes," Janos said,
"But it might just be the dogs." He set the table,
Shrugged. Janos was a friend from the university,
who fled east to join a people's liberation army,

died in Siberia somewhere. *Some of us whispered 'art'*
he said. *Some of us 'truth.' A debate with cut vocal cords.*
You have to understand that, for all we knew, the Germans
would be there forever. And if not the Germans, the Russians.
Well, you don't 'have to' understand anything, naturally.
No one knew which way to jump. What we had was language,
you see. Some said art, some said truth. Truth, of course,
was death. Clattered the plates down on the table. *No one,*
no one said 'self-expression.' Well, you had your own forms
of indulgence. Didn't people in the forties says 'man'
instead of 'the self?' I think I said. *I thought 'the self'*
came in in 1949. He laughed. *It's true. Man,*
we said, is the creature who is able to watch himself
eat his own shit from fear. You know what that is?
Melodrama. I tell you, there is no bottom to self-pity.

This comes back to me on the mountainside. Butterflies—
tiny blues with their two dot wings like quotation marks
or an abandoned pencil sketch of a face. They hover lightly
over lupine blooms, whirr of insects in the three o'clock sun.
What about being? I had asked him. *Isn't language responsible*
to it, all of it, the texture of bread, the hairstyles
of the girls you knew in high school, shoelaces, sunsets,
the smell of tea? Ah, he said, *you've been talking to Milosz.*
To Czeslaw I say this: silence precedes us. We are catching up.
I think he was quoting Jabes whom he liked to read.
Of course, here, gesturing out the window, pines, ragged green
of a winter lawn, the bay, *you can express what you like,*
enumerate the vegetation. And you! you have to, I'm afraid,
since you don't excel at metaphor. A shrewd, quick glance
to see how I have taken this thrust. *You write well, clearly.*
You are an intelligent man. But—finger in the air—
silence is waiting. Milosz believes there is a Word
at the end that explains. There is silence at the end,
and it does not explain, it asks. He spread chutney
on his bread, meticulously, out to the corners. Something
angry always in his unexpected fits of thoroughness
I liked. The cheese. Then a lunging, wolfish bite.
Put it this way, I give you, here, now, a magic key.
What does it open? This key I give you, what exactly

does it open? Anything, anything! But what? I found
that what I thought about was the failure of my marriage,
the three or four lost years just at the end and after.
For me there is no key, not even the sum total of our acts.
But you are a poet. You pretend to make poems. And?

She sat on the couch sobbing, her ribcage shaking
from its accumulated abysses of grief and thick sorrow.
I don't love you, she said. The terrible thing is
that I don't think I ever loved you. I thought to myself
fast, to numb it, that she didn't mean it, thought
what I had done to provoke it. It was May.
Also pines, lawn, the bay, a blossoming apricot.
Everyone their own devastation. Each on its own scale.
I don't know what the key opens. I know we die,
and don't know what is at the end. We don't behave well.
And there are monsters out there, and millions of others
to carry out their orders. We live half our lives
in fantasy, and words. This morning I am pretending
to be walking down the mountain in the heat.
A vault of blue sky, traildust, the sweet medicinal
scent of mountain grasses, and at the trailside—
I'm a little ashamed that I want to end this poem
singing, but I want to end this poem singing—the wooly
closed-down buds of the sunflower to which, in English,
someone gave the name, sometime, of pearly everlasting.

from *Colorado Review*

Heroin

◇　◇　◇

Imagine spring's thaw, your brother said,
each house a small rain, the eaves muttering
like rivers and you the white skin
the world sheds, your flesh unfolded

and absorbed. You walked Newark together,
tie loosened, a silk rainbow undone,
his fatigues the flat green of summer's end,
all blood drained from the horizon.

It would have been easier had you music
to discuss, a common love for one
of the brutal sports, if you shared
his faith that breath and sumac are more

alike than distinct, mutations of the same
tenacity. You almost tried it for him,
cinched a belt around your arm, aimed
a needle at the bloated vein, your window

open to July's gaunt wind and the radio
dispersing its chatty somnolence. When
he grabbed your wrist, his rightful face
came back for a moment: he was fifteen

and standing above Albert Ramos, fists
clenched, telling the boy in a voice
from the Old Testament what he'd do if certain
cruelties happened again. Loosening the belt,

you both walked out, straight and shaking,
into the hammering sun, talked of the past
as if it were a painting of a harvested field,
two men leaning against dusk and pitchforks.

That night he curled up and began to die,
his body a pile of ants and you on the floor
ripping magazines into a mound of words
and faces, touching his forehead with the back

of your hand in a ritual of distress, fading
into the crickets' metered hallucination.
When in two days he was human again, when
his eyes registered the scriptures of light,

when he tried to stand but fell and tried
again, you were proud but immediately
began counting days, began thinking
his name was written in a book

locked in the safe of a sunken ship,
a sound belonging to water, to history,
and let him go, relinquished him
to the strenuous work of vanishing.

from Indiana Review

California

◊　◊　◊

From the cool electric gaze of a Hollywood enigma
to the cormorant eating fish at a Muir Beach tide pool,
the state's a deep oasis of appetite and ease.
The newspaper reports eighty quakes a week,
most of them temblors faint as a star on water.
As whole hands of fog drape over the Golden Gate,
a piano in Oakland moans like a choir.
In the High Sierras, falling snow
is blue as brand-new skin;
the world's weight is measured
by a metaphysical Reno as clean as Disneyland.
Closer to Sacramento, the hum of BMWs
on their way to a software convention
sounds tasteful in the rain.
The motel owner knows the desert speed
of screenplays, since he is writing one
in the neon light of a nude but lucid room.
A postmodern bar just opened down the street.
No dancing, no smoking, no alcohol are allowed.
But you can get a mud bath, scented body wrap,
and whales hysterically singing
directly into your headphones.
The county sheriff has a Ph.D. and surfs the internet.
Relations are wreathed with chaos theory
and the "new world order."
       As the millennium approaches and nature
politely recedes, everyone thinks good thoughts.
Former cheerleaders join a women's drumming circle.
The family leaves the Methodist Church

for a sweat lodge in the country. In the absence
of the Soviet Union, Satan makes a comeback
along with angels who look like airline stewards,
cheeks rosy with steroids and purpose.
But they're on leave or out of work.
Narcissus drowns in a tide pool while reflecting
on a starfish; Sisyphus rides a mountain bike
up Mt. Tamalpais, where Zeus confuses omniscience
with his remote control. The future oversleeps.
But in a trailer home in Rancho Cucamonga,
the present has a theory scratched as paradise.
Bruise's star is dark.
        The bargain was to sing, as populations do,
the terrors of pleasure, like holding the gecko's tail
after it has dropped. Disguised by rear-view worlds,
we have taken steps in just that direction.
Glad the puritans came, we wander back repressed
to the land we would unsettle. Darkness
swallows borders. A wilderness shines.

from *The New Republic*

Helicopter Wrecked on a Hill

◊ ◊ ◊

Proving again that posture is everything,
you spin the illusion of rescue
and departure's threat, throned pilgrim.
You call yourself *turbine* and *windmill*
banking on science and nostalgia alternately
as you whine your way back into scenic routes,
a hollow and heroic riff.
Imagine the world's need for your remedy,
beginning life anew: a tail chasing
its dog, a push lawn mower turns over
its one fresh-cut gimmick.
Yet you wink like a plate licked clean
as your anchor unravels its line
and takes up the film reel of a plantation
of sophisticated blades. What they could do
to divide our view into slices
while wheeling it all together
with addition and multiplication crosses,
carrying all we believe.
With centrifugal bliss
you unscrew life-or-death promises
and whirl off your many veils
like shades of halos from your mounted,
swinging factory, cobra-coiling zeroes
like a lucky number or a tally
of wasted time and tired intent,

running up the bill while the wind
cannot be counted on to blow.
Still, the baton girl goes on, proud head
of the parade twirling her first rib,
giving and giving her gift to the good world.

from *Denver Quarterly*

The Butterfly Effect

◊ ◊ ◊

Think of it in Beijing,
the swallowtail on its white blossom.

Over there a man sleeps
beneath a bo tree.

A woman walks by a pond of red carp.
It is the last of September,

and the sky is clear all the way to the mountains.
No one sees the butterfly's wings move

nor feels the air stir
in the afternoon,

the small disturbance on the pond.
And when the swallowtail flies off

it is just a little more of the same,
a branch creaking, a ripple

over some geography like light over wheat,
except a month later,

thousands of miles away,
a wind knocks trees over,

it snows for days.
Children no longer turn somersaults.

Women turn away from sifting and measuring,
a man watches a deer stagger,

starving, across the frozen river.
The horizon hardly stirs,

and all the pianos are silent.
The bright wing of the sky

drifts so close you could raise a hand
to it, the air delicate

and your fingers itching a little,
as if something had landed there.

from *The Gettysburg Review*

Passacaglia

◊ ◊ ◊

You did it, didn't you?
I cannot occasion that from here.
Unplugged, I do not require conversation
to oppress what least I care for. I am playing Clue
for once, Xeroxing the crime I am not
to handlebar the invisible caress, the eaves
getting ready to sturdy my life, paranoid
about truth today. It is a gimlet, a spot remover
that depends on spills where gulls unfasten
their wives. To confess past that is enough.
To erase ceilings and to fence-post selfless
fragments of web with the help of wedding music
and friends.

Stomachs are full because there is hope,
not because history is a medical kit, a meditation
on stone, a spectrum thin as a rash. Let me begin
where I met you. Already the downplay slackens
and the accidental tension, the requests, like sawdust,
scent whatever it is that is unscented. In another time,
machines will be built to prove there is malice
and then wrong to care for such things.
Vision will include the sting in the eye, the particles
on tables where dinner should be but is not.

I am positioning myself, my work-songs away
from the loneliness that returns to doctor the clock.
Time is not time to some birds. The past is not chirping.
It chirped.

from *Colorado Review*

Making It Stick

◊ ◊ ◊

Asian American—
And ashamed of it;

I'm Asian—
But my owner's
Caucasian!

Model Minority On
Board

Ask me about
My GREEN CARD!

Don't blame me—
I'm a citizen!

Honk if you're
Sushi!

I'd rather be
Studying!

My child
are Student
of the
Yale!

Asian/Pacific
Islander
Gang Member!

Proud to be
Assimilated!

        We support
        Your troops!

                An old pond.
                A frog jumps in.
                The sound of water . . .

from *Many Mountains Moving*

The Poem That Was Once Called "Desperate" But Is Now Striving to Become the Perfect Love Poem

◇　◇　◇

So then the sunken heart was hauled up, nearly breaking
the nets, and just at that moment, back ashore,
while the scandalous flowers were opening to the sun,
while Agamemnon had finished sending his messages
of condolence to his wife, the somber moon
began to exert unusual control over this sentence,
and I thought, wait a minute, what if this poem worked
and she began to love me? What if I could invent
a new word the way Catullus invented a word
for kiss? And would I have time to change those stars
that have been embalmed in the eyes of Agamemnon
to something like— well, —but I know I *could*
think of something the way Clytemnestra's sentries
imagined every sunrise or glint of steel
to be the long awaited signal fire.
Sentries, secret messages, royal scandals,
who am I kidding? When am I going
to stop living off the debris of lost loves?

But if it was to work, the poem, shouldn't I stop
wasting time and talk about something more
important in order to make her love me? There's

the Clytemnestra syndrome to think about here
that is, the question of who lies best to whom.
And take Catullus, —in one of his poems to Lesbia,
he talks about Troy and Herakles just to let her know
how cultured he is— yes, the mind, despite what we think,
it's *that* important—and then he mentions his brother
who died in Turkey, and he really did mourn a lifetime
for him, but the point is, he lets Lesbia feel his remorse too,
then sympathy, then, —well, good sex, that was
Catullus' aim all along, wasn't it? And so with this
poem, surely there's time to add something about
my knowledge of the Trojan war, the complexities
concerning Agamemnon's murder of his daughter
and how I agree that, no matter how much the gods
commanded him, he should have turned around and
set sail for home and his anxious wife, all the while
emphasizing my essential sympathy with Clytemnestra's
plan to cut the bastard up like tonight's roast pork.

Maybe I should just go back to that little ship in the cove,
hauling up not a heart this time, but a statue, yes,
and an important find, good enough for a famous museum, —
but, well maybe not, museums mean the past, death, lost
civilizations, lost love, so maybe a treasure,—okay, ancient
Greek coins because this poem is set off some Greek isle,—
Agamemnon, remember— but wait, the trouble with dragging
in Agamemnon is that Aeschylus who wrote the play died
on just such a shore when an eagle dropped a shell on his head—
so maybe it's Sappho's island—this sticks better to my subtext—
where the poetess mourned for her lost love, and where—

But Sappho, you ask? Okay, true enough, but remember
Catullus also filled his poems with confusions of gender
to suggest the largesse of his sensitive and empathetic
vision to even the most difficult of lovers. Me too.
And why should I keep my hormones padlocked
in a single shed? Look what happened to Clytemnestra
waiting a decade for the one thing that drove her mad.
And why does everyone have to keep frisking the heart
for secret weapons? Why should I have to live like

there's an asterisk next to my love? Maybe the desperate
past is ready to weigh anchor, maybe my ideas are so plentiful
they'll just spill from the holes in my pockets like ancient
coins, and there she'll be, on that shore as the boat sails off,
happy like me, dressed like a Greek goddess, and she's ready
to spend a little time in my story, this story, with you
and me, where love is smuggled on board in containers
marked history, responsibility, prophecy, all those things
Desire's watchman never sees, decorum, reason, reality,
and all the other contraptions we use to try to avoid them.

from *The North American Review*

Dust Storm

◊ ◊ ◊

A secret like a lodestar, a ball of pure lead, I thought
about tasting him long enough for a life to wither,
a new planet to come into view. I imagined the smell
of his genitals, so common, so indescribable.
Wyoming and summer. Thunderheads galloping
in a stark yellow light. Or puffball clouds white
as eggs streaming over eye-piercing cobalt skies.
Grasses and hyssop. Jewelweed and coneflower.
Through the long evenings we would lean against
fences telling our lives more precisely than they had
ever been told. Desire rang bell-deep in my pelvic bone.
Two foxes looping along a ridge, or two coyotes.
Moon licked clean the sleek backs of his geldings.
Wherever I slept, my body spiraled then glided.
Distant ancestors appeared in dreams and spread
embroidered robes and silken scarves before me,
opened lacquered boxes filled with blue dust.
The prairie winds caught that dust. Even the crickets'
scrapings grew muted. One can over-think a thing.
The road skirled dust into tiny funnels, the funnels
to waves, the waves to a sea. I never slept with him,
but grew remote as a watch. Windswept plains,
sagebrush, tumbleweeds, and later, contrails
that crosshatched a shock-pink sky. His cattle
began to look painfully dumb. All were castrated.
My blood had grown too thin in Wyoming's thin air.
A woman out of her element, adrift on a high plateau.

from *Ploughshares*

Mud

◇　◇　◇

A bus driver from Delhi to Agra
says he plays tabla. Four of his fingers
are stumps, cut roughly above the knuckle.

I've got five children, he says,
and four who are no more. What happens
to our losses? Do they fly away, say,

like the green parakeet you let escape
into towering oaks while cleaning the cage
when you were six? Do they cling

to ponds on the underside of the cup, partially
hidden but warm? A carp floats gold
through the smoky Delhi sky, the shade

of a dead pig at dawn. Something is always
covered in mud. The scent of her
voice, the plaid of that wool skirt

she wore that rainy afternoon when she asked
for forgiveness, and you sat, silent,
drawing on a cigarette. A shift in polar light

can darken Bihar, make birds brittle
as water-buffalo chips set out to dry
on sides of huts. A gold, gold leaf falling through

a jungle floor is not gold, is not
the floor. An astronomer lecturing
on the merits of primitive star-charts

is not the night sky in a cave but a form
of grace body-bound but smart, caught
in the net of his mathematics. You draw

a hexagon in the mud and count
your failures. You count your fingers
to make sure. Mistakes blossom

like rare and familiar flowers, hot-house blood,
huge piles of gravel at the roadside
steaming like fresh bones from a hunt.

You want off the bus. You want to drown
yourself in the stagnant monsoon
pools of a rice field, smother in warm

water-buffalo shit, witness for yourself
a gherao, where the workers finally unite,
surround the evil landowner like a ring

of musk oxen, and threaten him
with spears of asparagus.
But all you see are those women

who carry huge gravel pans
on their heads, who report pelvic
pressure in their early 30s

from walking up and down
stone stairs balancing heavy pails
of milk, whose babies thirst for wood

and glimpse at birth the flight
of a green parakeet, the texture of oaks.
Something's always having its way

in mud, hidden in the crack in the gourd
of the sitar you bought in Benares, stitched
in the tabla's goatskin, gripping

the steering wheel of a bus and guiding it
all the way from Delhi to Agra to Delhi,
through the heat, through star-lit holes.

With the four lost souls of one's
youth. With the shade of her skirt
and scent of wet wool, even now—years later—

when you reach to touch your wife. With a tip
of asparagus freshly pulled from mud,
no longer hidden and harmless, but real.

from *New Letters*

The Bright Light
of Responsibility

◊ ◊ ◊

My friend said, "Let's go down to the river.
Bosses from all over the state are having sex with their young secretaries
in a wild group fucking kind of office thing with prosthetics and elec-
     tricity.
They're misusing whipped cream can chargers and animal sedatives.
The press is invited and nobody's going to get in trouble."
I told her, "No! I won't go. It's not right.
Even if these big fat men get interviewed on *Entertainment Tonight*
and they never get in trouble and this fancy paparazzi butthole rim job
propels every hoochie mama participant into some star-studded model-
     ing career,
it's still not right.
Getting on top of someone in public is wrong."
Then my friend said, "OK then. Let's go crazy and not shower for a
     month.
Then we get on the city bus for $1.25 and wet our pants.
It'll smell terrible and make people incredibly nervous,
but no one will ask us any questions and we won't get in trouble."
Well I told her, "Hey, no! It's not right.
God invented hygiene to serve mankind.
Urine belongs inside of you, not on public transportation.
No one would ask you any questions
because talking to someone who wets their pants on a city bus
is like talking to a space invader from Mars.
People are afraid you might flick pee at them or something and ruin
     their lives."

Then my friend said, "OK Miss God-Almighty-Hot-Pants-Goes-To-
        Church,
what say we give up regular food like macaroni and tomatoes,
forget we ever ate them, and concentrate on vending machines:
your Funyuns, your Mello Yello, your Tootsie Rolls,
your Cherry Pepsi, your Now and Laters, your Pepperoni Combos.
We eat nothing but that for the entirety of our formative years
and well into adulthood. Then we complain about our teeth,
how they're all rotten, and lift up our lips to show our co-workers the
        holes.
Then we buy some guns.
We force Asian tourists at gunpoint
to look at our holes. Then we say, 'We don't care.
We'll just get them all pulled out,' and we won't get in trouble, OK?"
I told her, "OK my eye! It is no OK! It's not right.
The four food groups are for everybody.
Vegetables are not optional.
You cannot substitute Pringles for rice.
People! All teeth start out just fine
and then you go and fill them full of holes.
It's not like a car accident.
A person drives all the cars in the city that is their mouth.
You build the roads.
You elect the public officials—
they will even wear what you tell them to wear.
If you really like stupid silver platform boots and empire waist baby
        doll dresses
then that is what the mayor will wear to his inaugural dinner
and every day for the rest of his life.
It's all yours, and leaving non-English speakers free
to wander around in rental cars,
up to God knows what kind of crap, unchecked, is madness!
Forget it. I know—let's go get 10 of those big green tropical cocktails
instead and see who can drink theirs the fastest.
I'll drive."
"OK," she said
and together we walked out into the bright light of responsibility.

from *Exquisite Corpse*

A Bill, Posted

◇　◇　◇

Lost: black bible in case, Chicago address. Please call . . .

It's a limited edition given out by the Gideons
before they went green and small. The title page inscription
reads "to my wife with Love," and there's a photo
of our daughter marking an Epistle of Paul. Of course,
we can talk reward but nothing above fifty dollars.
I'm not a railroad exec nor do I own a granary.
And the hog business is one that is alien to me.
I was on an El the day I realized the book was gone.
Mesmerized by the buildings passing by, the train
nearly burrowing through them, I noticed a kitten
on a window ledge with the same expression
on its face. She was caught in the reflection
in the glass: some men around an oil barrel fire,
one a cop, the others just regulars of the downtown,
not talking or motioning, simply staring
at the coil of flame. They were meditating upon
the ashes and stirring them. Their ashes. On my way
to another job interview. I did not take heed
of their inaction, but like the animal, was entrapped
in the vision of a vision. The tracks lulled me
with their minimal attempt at music. The clouds
promised danger—low flying scud, the stratosphere
a grey blanket over the grey city. My umbrella:
a walking stick in between the occasional bouts of showers.
Another ordinary day preceded by lake front
and slouching store fronts. Skeletons of dwellings

bordering the curves of our route. A young man
impeccably dressed offered me directions and a station
stop from where to depart, the best place to reach
the northern spread of the metropolis. I must have
carried the air of a tourist, being in a daze, rubber-necked
and wearing my trousers rolled. He tipped his hat
as he left and tucked his paper under arm, his good deed
card punched for the day. But I continued on,
past the elegant light posts just beginning to illumine.
The Chrysalis tavern had patrons waiting at its door.
I wished mightily for a plug of tobacco with which
I could smoke an Abd-el-Kadir pipe. My pockets
were filled with small specie and keys that mean nothing
to me until their destined doors; one being the apartment,
the others the locked boxes filled with papers,
my collection of ancient coins, and one securely hidden
that holds the secret not even my wife knows about:
a pistol my grandfather handed down from the war.
Once, I had a bottle of chloroform with which I could
subdue butterflies. Its shards still twinkle in the alley
where our daughter dropped it after putting the neighbor's
puppy out for a spell. I know now well there are
things we all need to keep personal. My wife occasionally
wears a former lover's brooch and I do not hold this against her.
I think this too is why when I rode the city's newest toy,
the elevator lift, the people on board remained silent.
Who knows what could happen behind those closed doors?
At the predestined exit, I took my leave, a crow bickering
with the wind reminded me I needed to get some pumpernickel
at the Polish bakery. The people inside already queued
reminded me by their sudden quietude that I was not
of their rugged stock. Some kielbasa would be nice
if we could afford it. The southbound took me
back home and it was then, on the slower train,
that I realized I was without my cherished book.
I save the Lamentations always for the return
after another long day looking for work. The new-
fangled one I kept from a hotel in Ohio won't do—
I feel lost without my book I've kept from school
with our priest's inscription on the back cover.

It is the holy relic I cut my teeth on, so to say.
I so hope the advertisements I posted in the train
will suffice. They contain my telephone number,
an address, the simple enumerations of my life.

from *Poetry*

Jeanne Duval's Confession

◇ ◇ ◇

Because Charles couldn't
   dare beyond my breasts
     & berry-colored lips

saying "Madame est
   servie" in a short play,
     I never stopped seeing him

as some bouffant boy,
   with an armload of roses
     outside that stage door,

petals in Paris snow.
   Locked in his Babel
     of books, he quizzed himself

till he was nothing
   but a diseased root,
     till I was a whore

& Black Madonna,
   not a real woman
     beneath conjured cloth

& sheer lackluster.
   It wasn't my idea
     to garnish an apartment

with a blonde maid.
  I became Beatrice
   & Hamlet's mother

seduced with tropic fruit
  between a lion's den
   & paradise. A bemused

lament, a brown body,
  a good luck charm
   found on Friday

the thirteenth. "Obi,
  Faustus . . . ebony thighs,
   child of midnights. . . ."

Charles tried to work me
  out of his heart & spleen,
   but I'd been made into

a holy wild perfume,
  a vertigo of bells in his head,
   the oboe's mouth-hole

licked with opium.
  A Haitian cock bristled
   beneath my shoulder blades,

& only gold coins
  could calm me down.
   The most precious litany

dripped from his melancholy
  quill. Even his red-haired
   beggar girl possessed

my breasts. Charles
  was hexed from head to toe,
   but it wasn't my fault.

His mother said she
　　burned my letters because
　　　　I never said I loved

her son. He tried
　　to erase what he'd created
　　　　by mouthing Latin verses

beneath Wagner's piano.
　　As I leaned in an alley
　　　　on my crutches, behind

a pie shop, halfway
　　to a pauper's grave, it was
　　　　then he seized a last breath

because I couldn't stop
　　saying how much I loved
　　　　a man who could kill with words.

　　　from *Black Warrior Review*

ELIZABETH KOSTOVA

Suddenly I Realized
I Was Sitting

◊ ◊ ◊

I was entirely—let me start again. I was entirely unsure how the situation. I was entirely unsure how the situation arose out of nothing. As situations do. First, you think you know people: Rose, Phil, that other acquaintance who knows both of them. Then you're looking through them, through their quirks—like handling a pen badly, complaining about minor illnesses, tipping too little at restaurants because they can't do arithmetic. You're not only seeing through them, but hearing through them, almost not hearing them, almost not hearing what you're listening to. One is telling a story, already too long a story for a short lunch. One is telling a story you've heard before from another friend. Listening, looking, seeing through them as if they are becoming transparent around the table, you are there but not present to them, you are watching. Suddenly I realized I was sitting on a volcano. First, the friends around me, then the situation looming up large and solid, bulky under or beyond their insubstantial forms. And what is it? Rose loves. No. Phil hates Rose from way back. No. You can't name it but it's there, the volcano, the unloving or too-loving mass of situation. You'd make a plot of it. Frightening, maybe, or dull or worth trying to describe, but always something. Not always volcano. Not always. In this case, however, I realized suddenly that I was sitting on.

from *Another Chicago Magazine*

The Change

◇   ◇   ◇

For years the dead
were the terrible weight of their absence,
the weight of what one had not put in their hands.
Rarely a visitation—dream or vision—
lifted that load for a moment, like someone
standing behind one and briefly taking
the heft of a frameless pack.
But the straps remained, and the ache—
though you can learn not to feel it
except when malicious memory
pulls downward with sudden force.
Slowly there comes a sense
that for some time the burden
has been what you need anyway.
How flimsy to be without it, ungrounded, blown
hither and thither, colliding with stern solids.
And then they begin to return, the dead:
but not as visions. They're not
separate now, not to be seen, no,
it's they who see: they displace,
for seconds, for minutes, maybe longer,
the mourner's gaze with their own. Just now,
that shift of light, arpeggio
on ocean's harp—
not the accustomed bearer
of heavy absence saw it, it was perceived

by the long-dead, long absent, looking
out from within one's wideopen eyes.

from *Seneca Review*

Anastasia and Sandman

◊　◊　◊

The brow of a horse in that moment when
The horse is drinking water so deeply from a trough
It seems to inhale the water, is holy.

I refuse to explain.

When the horse had gone, the water in the trough,
All through the empty summer,

Went on reflecting clouds & stars.

The horse cropping grass in a field,
And the fly buzzing around its eyes, are more real
Than the mist in one corner of the field.

Or the angel hidden in the mist, for that matter.

Members of the Committee on the Ineffable,
Let me illustrate this with a story, & ask you all
To rest your heads on the table, cushioned,
If you wish, in your hands, &, if you want,
Comforted by a small carton of milk
To drink from, as you once did, long ago,
When there was only a curriculum of beach grass,
When the University of Flies was only a distant humming.

In Romania, after the war, Stalin confiscated
The horses that had been used to work the fields.
"You won't need horses now," Stalin said, cupping

His hand to his ear, "Can't you hear the tractors
Coming in the distance? I hear them already."
The crowd in the Callea Victoria listened closely
But no one heard anything. In the distance
There was only the faint glow of a few clouds.
And the horses were led into boxcars & emerged
As the dimly remembered meals of flesh
That fed the starving Poles
During that famine, & part of the next one—
In which even words grew thin & transparent,
Like the pale wings of ants that flew
Out of the oldest houses, & slowly
What had been real in words began to be replaced
By what was not real, by the not exactly real.
"Well, not exactly, but . . ." became the preferred
Administrative phrasing so that the man
Standing with his hat in his hands would not guess
That the phrasing of a few words had already swept
The earth from beneath his feet. "That horse I had,
He was more real than any angel,
The housefly, when I had a house, was real too,"
Is what the man thought.
Yet it wasn't more than a few months
Before the man began to wonder, talking
To himself out loud before the others,
"Was the horse real? Was the house real?"
An angel flew in and out of the high window
In the factory where the man worked, his hands
Numb with cold. He hated the window and the light
Entering the window and he hated the angel.
Because the angel could not be carved into meat
Or dumped into the ossuary & become part
Of the landfill at the edge of town,
It therefore could not acquire a soul,
And resembled in significance nothing more
Than a light summer dress when the body has gone.

The man survived because, after a while,
He shut up about it.

Stalin had a deep understanding of the *kulaks,*
Their sense of marginalization & belief in the land,

That is why he killed them all.

Members of the Committee on Solitude, consider
Our own impoverishment & the progress of that famine,
In which, now, it is becoming impossible
To feel anything when we contemplate the burial,
Alive, in a two hour period, of hundreds of people.
Who were not clichés, who did not know they would be
The illegible blank of the past that lives in each
Of us, even in some guy watering his lawn

On a summer night. Consider
The death of Stalin & the slow, uninterrupted
Evolution of the horse, a species no one,
Not even Stalin, could extinguish, almost as if
What could not be altered was something
Noble in the look of its face, something

Incapable of treachery.

Then imagine, in your planning proposals,
The exact moment in the future when an angel
Might alight & crawl like a fly into the ear of a horse,
And then, eventually, into the brain of a horse,
And imagine further that the angel in the brain
Of this horse, is, for the horse cropping grass
In the field, largely irrelevant, a mist in the corner
Of the field, something that disappears,
The horse thinks, when weight is passed through it,
Something that will not even carry the weight
Of its own father
On its back, the horse decides, & so demonstrates
This by swishing at a fly with its tail, by continuing
To graze as the dusk comes on & almost until it is night.

Old contrivers, daydreamers, walking chemistry sets,
Exhausted chimneysweeps of the spaces

Between words, where the Holy Ghost tastes just
Like the dust it is made of,
Let's tear up our lecture notes & throw them out
The window.
Let's do it right now before wisdom descends on us
Like a spiderweb over a burned out theatre marquee,
Because what's the use?
I keep going to meetings where no one's there,
And contributing to the discussion;
And besides, behind the angel hissing in its mist
Is a gate that leads only into another field,
Another outcropping of stones & withered grass, where
A horse named Sandman & a horse named Anastasia
Used to stand at the fence & watched the traffic pass.
Where there were outdoor concerts once, in summer,
Under the missing & innumerable stars.

from *The American Poetry Review*

Hallelujah Terrible

◇   ◇   ◇

No other man has come down that way with his foot so big
and his eyes so blue
as if the last thing he wanted to do was come down with his foot
and feel the beginning of earth
run through his leg.

No other man wanted to scream that way before the sun went down
and the rain began in his underwear at the foothills
opened mouth before the owl and hawk and other bird circling above
that dead thing in roadway called godfoot.

Who must know the pulse of two baby girls on the factory floor
upset and upbeat before the whistles blow sounding mmmmmmm?

Nothing else is as beautiful as the other man putting his fist
through two planks of wood so large the timber men come for him
for consultation on the last state of the trees.
The trees are real.
That is their state.
They holler mom.

There are no other men in the shower washing their arms
for godsakes the arms so dark there are nights coming in close
for comfort
and stars wandering past other stars looking for help.
The help is in the blood.
The blood is as you expect.
See it leak from his knuckles above the sink. Stain the sink.
So jewel-like and unlike anything

that might exist in any part of the universe swirling this way
and into corners.

No other man has blood as blue as sky in September
before the angels choke on foliage and the trees blast off
singing hallelujah hallelujah terrible terrible hallelujah.

from *Seneca Review*

Empress of Sighs

◇ ◇ ◇

Mom says getting to the new home is a snap. "As easy as a cake falling off a log on a bicycle." Just take a left on Palm Canyon until you reach Desert Falls, bear left at the fork of Indian Canyon and Canyon Plaza taking Desert Canyon to Canyon Sands. This is where you will find Rancho La Paz. Click on 2 for the gate, the guard waves you past and you're on Avenida del Sol where you continue on crossing Vista del Sol, Plaza del Sol, Vista del Monte, Sunny Dunes, Camino Parocela—make sure you heed the golf cart crossing—and then Thousand Palms, Emerald Desert, Desert Isle and Palm Desert Greens. Left on Sagewood, right on Sungate, left on Palo Verde, and ending in the cul-de-sac of Casa La Paz.

"I just love it," Mom says.

"You love it?" I say.

"Yes. I love it!" Then she calls to dad who's enjoying himself on the 18-hole putting green located just 3 feet outside the kitchen sliding glass door, "Don't we love it, hon?"

He tips the brim of his white cap, a cap he would have seen on someone a year ago and called them a fag and says, "Love it! Another crappy day in paradise! Ha! Ha! Ha!"

Mom clears her throat a little and sighs. She is the Empress of Sighs. "Well, yes, it's still a little funny."

Same funny tax bracket, same funny year round tans, same funny cathedral ceilings. Same politics, same stocks, same paranoia and medication. The same leather interior, glossy exterior and liposuctioned posterior.

Here comes your neighbor driving up in a luxury sedan just like your luxury sedan except he paid extra for the little headlight wipers and the gold linked license plate frame—and you didn't. You thought they were useless, extraneous, a little much . . . and now your neighbor comes rubbering by, waving real slow, doing the grown-up equivalent of "ha-ha!" which is basically "ha-ha! I am worth more than you."

And Mom sighs and admits it doesn't feel like home yet.

This mom, Empress of Sighs, Empress of afterschool treats and frumpy sweaters and marathon tickling and the 52 Casseroles cookbook, doesn't feel at home.

So I map out a plan. I make a list on how one feels at home here. I say, you need to play bridge, throw a party, plan on some tennis and it'll feel like home. Polish the silver, throw out old photos, balance your checkbook, it'll feel like home. Start eating more fresh fruit. Get your armpits waxed. Drink 6 8oz. glasses of water each day. It'll feel like home.

Squeeze all your blackheads, clip toenails in bed, watch 13 straight hours of television. Complain about what trash they show on television and begin writing a letter. Stop writing the letter cause it makes you think about yourself, yell at your mother instead, quit drinking. Threaten to deport the gardener.

Go on a crying jag. Consider rhinoplasty, blepharoplasty and a tummy tuck. Forget to water the plants. Buy plastic plants and forget to dust them. Buy books and pretend you read them. Start a collection. Start a collection of something that might be worth something someday.

Now turn off the lights, sprawl out on one of the matching earthtoned leather sofas and pick a very high number. Start counting backwards. You're in the middle of the desert, the wind picks up and when you run out of numbers, you will find that it feels a lot like home.

from *Clockwatch Review*

135

Heartsong

◇ ◇ ◇

A bird sings from the tree. The birds sing
sending waves of desire—and I stand on my roof
waiting for a randomness to storm my days. I stand on my roof
filled with the longing that sings its way out of the bird.
And I am afraid that my call will break me,
that the cry blocked by my tongue will pronounce me mad.
O bird mad with longing, O balancing bar,
tightrope, monkey grunting from a roof. Fortunate bird.
I stand on my roof and wave centuries of desire.
I am the Bedouin pondering the abandoned campsite
licking the ashes of the night fire; the American walking
walking miles of dresses, blouses, and skirts
filling them with infinite lovers;
the mystic feeling the pull swirling in his chest,
a desert of purpose expanding and burning and yellowing
every shade of green. And I stand on my roof.
And I say come like a stranger, like a feather
falling on an old woman's shoulder, like a hawk
that comes to feed from her hands, come like a mystery,
like sunlight rain, a blessing, a bus falling off a bridge,
come like a deserting soldier, a murderer chased by law,
like a girl prostitute escaping her pimp, come like a lost horse,
like a dog dying of thirst, come love, come ragged and melancholy
like the last day on earth, come like a sigh from a sick man,
come like a whisper, like a bump on the road, like a flood,
a dam braking, turbines falling from the sky,
come love like the stench of a swamp, a barrage of light
filling a blind girl's eye, come like a memory
convulsing the body into sobs, like a carcass floating on a stream,

come like a vision, come love like a crushing need,
come like an afterthought. Heart song. Heart song.
The pole smashes and the live wires yellow streaks
on the lush grass. Come look and let me wonder.
Someone. So many. The sounds of footsteps, horses and cars.
Come look and let me wonder. And I stand on my roof
echoing the bird's song and the world says: Do not sleep.
Do not sleep now that you have housed your longing
within the pain of words.

from *Ploughshares*

Vermin

◇ ◇ ◇

"What do you want to be when you grow up?"
What child cries out, "An exterminator!"?
One diligent student in Mrs. Taylor's
class will get an ant farm for Christmas, but
he'll not see industry; he'll see dither.
"The ant sets an example for us all,"
wrote Max Beerbohm, a master of dawdle,
"but it is not a good one." These children
don't hope to outlast the doldrums of school
only to heft great weights and work in squads
and die for their queen. Well, neither did we.
And we knew what we didn't want to be:
the ones we looked down on, the lambs of God,
blander than snow and slow to be cruel.

from *The New Yorker*

JOSIP NOVAKOVICH

Shadow

◊　◊　◊

My son had a hard time learning the concept of shadow. At first, to him every puddle of oil in the road was a shadow, and I did not tell him that he was wrong, for maybe he wasn't. The oil may be a shadow fragment of a herd of dead zebras; the oil puddle may be a shadow of a bad engine. Maybe my son thought that we leaked out our shadows in some kind of dark liquid that could dry quickly as soon as we stepped aside, and another leak would form instantly in the new place. He once grabbed my bag full of books and dragged it in circles, shouting, This is my shadow! I did not tell him that he was wrong, for maybe he wasn't. The books could be shadows of a herd of dead writers, dragged on the floor, like Hector around Troy; and maybe the books were the shadow of my son's future reading and strained eyes. Now he understands what a shadow is more conventionally. That's you, Daddy, he says, and points at my shadow. That's Joey, he says, and points at his shadow. In the morning, our shadows are long and thin; at lunchtime, they are short and fat. Shadows are never alone; we keep them company. When the sun is up, maybe my son is my shadow; and at sunset, maybe the shadow he casts down in the gravel is me—it is as long as me. We are our shadows. The sun casts us as shadows. Our flesh is the engine for forming the puddles, us, in the road. When the sun is gone, we are out. Shadowless. Or maybe then I'm an unaccompanied shadow, a celloless unaccompaniment. My son wakes up when there's light, and says, Daddy, the sun is up, get up!—and we stand up to make more shadows. He makes them by being an obstacle to the light's path. And I spread onto the dust at the speed of darkness.

from *Another Chicago Magazine*

From *A Summer Evening*

◇   ◇   ◇

6:40

Toward the substation in the testing wind.
The trucks with ice inside their metal melting upcountry.
In the afternoon the sun is heartless.
In the evening the sun is a scientist.
"And God was feeling his enclosure."
The fields are usual and beige.
They evoke in people everywhere a sense of strange peace.
The trucks haul green bananas.
Each one has a dark nipple just for somebody, anybody.
Instead of good night we say "night heron."

11:15

Sun vibrates even on the umbles.
In strange peace a lieutenant's sleep.
After rain the gold-of-pleasure grows.
It is a member of the mustard family.
Who would sit in the ice-house regretting.
The sly-boots hiding in the dirty wind.
With his complicated plan involving herons.
Sun scientific in a yellow haze.
The hiding place a mix of fields and buildings.
Under the night sky the night module.

10:33

The lake he was generating while he slept.
Once in your lifetime, you must travel to Mecca.
Or stand up with water all over you.
Or willingly accept an animal to walk with you all through the woods.
The forest generated pandas and destroyed them.
And phlox was rotting in a large field of phlox after heavy rain.
So summer soaked and burned the Earth.
So Earth spun, in love, its own Mecca.
Meanwhile, these industrial cities sleep, extreme in red, red lakes.
Obedience.

8:49

Being somewhere else his limbs deadened.
The sect was stacks of calendars.
The grass widows cried, kneeling by the photographs.
In the vitrine, gold bars melted, grass grew complicated.
His janissary wandered around in the high grass and hid things.
They boiled scissors in the red rooms made of cinderblock.
The world is not round, it is more beautiful than that, a kind of blue gas.
There will be seven days of gaiety.
And by the 8th day we will inherit the katydid.
Taurus will give us a round, new planet.

from *Denver Quarterly*

Mostly Mick Jagger

◇ ◇ ◇

1

Thank god he stuck his tongue out.
When I was twelve I was in danger
of taking my body seriously.
I thought the ache in my nipple was priceless.
I thought I should stay very still
and compare it to a button,
a china saucer,
a flash in a car side-mirror,
so I could name the ache either big or little,
then keep it forever. He blew no one a kiss,
then turned into a maw.

After I saw him, when a wish moved in my pants,
I nurtured it. I stalked around my room
kicking my feet up just like him, making
a big deal of my lips. I was my own big boy.
I wouldn't admit it then,
but he definitely cocks his hip
as if he is his own little girl.

2

People ask me—I make up interviews
while I brush my teeth—*So, what do you remember best
about your childhood?* I say
mostly the drive toward Chicago.

Feeling as if I'm being slowly pressed against the skyline.
Hoping to break a window.
Mostly quick handfuls of boys' skin.
Summer twilights that took forever to get rid of.
Mostly Mick Jagger.

3

How do I explain my hungry stare?
My Friday night spent changing clothes?
My love for travel? I rewind the way he says *now*
with so much roof of the mouth.
I rewind until I get a clear mental image of myself:
I'm telling the joke he taught me
about my body. My mouth is stretched open
so I don't laugh. My hands are pretending
to have just discovered my own face.
My name is written out in metal studs
across my little pink jumper.
I've got a mirror and a good idea
of the way I want my face to look.
When I glance sideways, my smile should twitch
as if a funny picture of me is taped up
inside the corner of my eye.
A picture where my hair is combed over each shoulder,
my breasts are well supported, and my teeth barely show.
A picture where I'm trying hard to say *beautiful*.

He always says *this is my skinny rib cage,*
my one, two chest hairs.
That's all he ever says.
Think of a bird with no feathers
or think of a hundred lips bruising every inch of his skin.
There are no pictures of him hoping
he said the right thing.

from *The Cream City Review*

Valediction

◇ ◇ ◇

Your Mozart is not my Mozart anymore.
That hour has passed,
The harmony that thrilled us, the false sun
We warmed to. Your days are yours now
To pile up like dry leaves in your past, from which my past

Has broken off, diverged, gone
Into another woods altogether. No, I cannot make my way over
To you, to touch your face or other parts, not even those whose ache
I can feel at the great distance
That has fallen between us like a world.

I have measured the hours and days since we touched.
Each one healed as I handled it. In them grew this voice, still singing
Out of doubt and longing, a stricken sound.

You are struck from the record. Your hand, absolved
Of my flagrant touch. Dismantle the room
Where we've become marble figures, a white
Sculptured kiss, where we sat listening
To your Mozart, not mine.

from *Poetry*

Topophilia

◊ ◊   ◊ ?

I was going to ardently pursue this day
but you know how these things go.
I am a Hun and the sun is my chieftain
and chieftains are as they appear to their Huns . . .
So, sunless, I go from being a sleepy angel wearing god's toga
to a woman in a bathrobe wandering around a well-appointed house.
The transformations are astonishing; like a birch in April
the blood rushes to my head, only it's not April
and all the signs say don't go too soon, don't go too far,
don't even pass. The birch stands still and these things
are of some consequence in the country. And a domineering
little bird has eaten all the seeds. I think one day
it will build its nest in my abandoned cranium.
I study nature so as not to do foolish things.
For instance, in the worst windstorms
only the most delicate things survive:
a vireo's nest intact on the lawn next to the roots
of a monstrous tree. Life makes so much sense!
There goes the coach. The coach is of real gold
and the new queen is in it. I like trips, I book them all,
and I'm one of the lucky: my memories are actually finer
than those of those who go. I suspect the queen is going
to the despot's private party where they shove sweetmeats
down your decolletage and have a goose so slowly roasted
the poor bird cries whenever you pull off a piece
and everyone shrieks with joy. What does the outer world
know of the inner? It's like listening to wolves or loons . . .
Here comes the snow, that ought to make the children

happy as parrots flying over a gorge with a bamboo bridge
built like a xylophone and fruit bats hanging upsidedown
who look at the world and decide to go airy in ardent pursuit
of a plum. But what does the inner world know
of the outer? And will I find out soon? That word,
that word has kept me company all my life.

from *The American Poetry Review*

Recruiting Poster

◊   ◊   ◊

Oh, be more than you can be.
If one-eyed, then Cyclops or locomotive;
lame, Hephaestus or Somerset in Rome.
Be Groucho to the proud, Beppo to the silver-
tongued, Harpo to the remote and suave.
Oh, be what needs be otherwise.
If true, then fickle; fickle, true.
If omnicompetent, then forgetful;
forgetful, secretive; secretive,
spendthrift; spendthrift, omnicompetent.
Be a morass to the mighty,
a real wrench in the works:
bollix the Hubble constant,
bungle entropy botch the continental
drift. Be what hasn't occurred to you:
avalanche of elbows, hail larger than brainpans.
Be intrusive as a lunar flare,
reflective as copper double suns.
Be what kind Horatio neither had nor heard
in his philosophy and Riemann never subtended:
a brilliant mediocrity, an uninvited middle,
benighted, unbehooved.
Oh hell, be all you cannot be:
basilisk feverish with FM,
manticore mad with Malto-Meal, anything
not merely more but wholly else.
Be supernal. Be strangely absent.
Be what comes before, unentailed.

Be what or who or where
ever, but be torrid.
Oh, be most, then more so, then beyond.

from *Shenandoah*

Fiddleheads

◇   ◇   ◇

The first time I saw hundreds of fiddlehead ferns boiling in an enor-
    mous pot I realized
what an odd person I must be to hear tiny cries from the mouths of
    cooking vegetables.

Similarly, when you hurt me, I curled like a mouse behind my third eye.
    I realize what an
odd thing it is to believe as I do in my third eye and the mouse behind it
    that furls like a fern

and whimpers like a fern being boiled on a monster stove beside its
    brothers and sisters.
Poor mouse. The things that make a person odd are odd themselves.
    Think of DNA,

the way it resembles the rope Jack climbed to secure his future and that
    of his aging Mom.
Or the way a sudden wave can drag a child under, that addiction to
    adrenalin, her

siblings farther away and more powerless than she ever imagined, the
    pure and ecstatic
irreversibility of undertow. It's odd to come back to life, as they say, she
    came back to life.

I think I'll come back to life now. It's odd to think of something so big we
    could miss
the elephant we're living on, like this planet Earth, is she alive and we're
    her brain cells,

each one of us flickering, going out, coming back to life? Even Chicago
      looks poignant
from the top of the Hancock, organized and sincere. Think if we were
      photographing

Earth, how dear she would be, how we'd watch her shimmer in the
      shimmering black soup
of the firmament, how alone she'd look and how we'd long to protect
      her, the way it feels

to protect a woman at the height of orgasm, the liquid giving, the
      seawater slide of coming
back to life. When you hurt me, I evolved like a backboned sea creature,
      translucent

nervous system sparking along in the meanest deep where I was small
      enough to not care
and my passions ran to swimming, gulping, spitting bubbles back into
      new oceans.

Once when you hurt me I slept at a Red Roof Inn. I double-locked the
      door and tried to
watch Arsenio and keep my mind off sounds like someone suffocating
      someone

in the next room. I thought I saw blood on the boxspring and imagined
      needles and bulgy
veins, there's something odd, I thought, about someone whose
      imagination runs that wild.

So often I dream you're here and I wake in the middle of a prayer from
      my muzzled
childhood. *Jesus Mary and Joseph,* I say, appalled that I'm stuck in 1955
      when I need

something profane and 90's to see me through. Like Serrano's cross. Like
      ginger tea.
Like the idea that we're moving between horizons and the Earth is so
      wise she sends us

Autumn and red-tailed hawks when we least expect them. *I can do this,*
    I say,
and the planet shifts imperceptibly. From a great distance she appears
    to be at peace.

from *Green Mountains Review*

VIJAY SESHADRI

Lifeline

◊ ◊ ◊

As soon as he realized he was lost, that
in kicking around his new job in his head,
the new people he'd met, and how
he could manage a week in Seaside,
he'd stumbled past the muddy fork of road
that slithered down in switchbacks
to Highway 20, and now couldn't tell,
through rainclouds coarse as pig iron,
and about as cold, which languished
over each of the scarred mountaintops,
where west was, or east, or north,
or feel the sun's direction,
he stopped, as he knew he should,
and doubled back. An hour at the worst
would bring him to the International
inert in a ditch with its radiator
punctured, its axle broken, and blood
from his temple on the steering wheel.
He wished he'd never set eyes on that truck . . .
here he was, trudging like an idiot
through a thousand-square-mile dead spot
of Douglas fir, soaked to the bone
and hungry, with his head throbbing.
He wasn't up to this, he said to himself,
staring disconsolately outward
to the numberless ridges and valleys, singed
with the bitter green of the firs.
But why hadn't he reached the truck yet,
or at least somewhere familiar,

where he could get his bearings again?
He didn't recognize the ridge he was on.
He'd never seen this particular patch—
glinting with wild crocus prongs—
of clear-cut ground, torched and scarified.
Should he keep going, or return again?
There and then he made his third mistake.
Hearing, or thinking he heard,
deep in the valley below him plunged
in mist, a chain saw start and sputter,
he made off down toward the sound.
It would be a gypo logger, scrounging
deadfall cedar for shake-bolt cords,
or a civilian with a twenty-dollar permit
to cut firewood for sale at a roadside stand.
Either way, he could get directions
and hitch home by dark. Hours later,
night found him in a hollow, shouting
until he was hoarse for someone, anyone.
The weekend was almost here, and no one
at work would miss him before Monday . . .
he lived alone, idiot, he lived alone
and couldn't count on a single person
to send out an alarm. Those first hours
he spent shivering under a lip of rock,
wide awake, startling at each furtive,
night-hunting animal sound, each flap
of the raptors in the branches overhead.
On the second day he lost his glasses.
It happened like this: As he struggled
over the cryptic terrain all morning—
terrain that would seem, if looked at
from high above, from a helicopter
or a plane flying low enough to pierce
the dense, lazy foliage of clouds,
created, finessed, meticulously contrived
to amaze, like a marvellous relief map
of papier-mâché, revealing its artifice only
in the improbable dramas of its contours,
its extravagant, unlikely colors—

he had what amounted to a real insight.
All this was the brainchild of water.
Stretching back beyond the Pleistocene—
how many millions of years?—
imperial rain had traced without pity,
over and over again, its counter-image
on the newborn, jagged mountains
until the length of the coast had been
disciplined to a system on purpose designed
to irrigate and to nourish the soil.
He decided he'd follow the water down.
He'd use each widening tributary
like the rung of a ladder, to climb down
from his awful predicament, and soon
work his way to the ocean—though, of course,
long before that he'd run across people.
With this in mind, he came to a stream
heavy and brown with the spring runoff,
its embankment on his side steep
to the point of perpendicularity, thick
with brush, though on the other side
a crown of ferns tumbled gently down
to the next watershed. It seemed like
a good idea to cross, and farther on
he found a logged fir with a choker cable
still attached (it must have snapped
when they tried to yard the falled tree
to the road high above) straddling
the stream. A little more than halfway over
he slipped on the treacherous wood
and would have gone in but for the cable
which he lunged at just in time.
That was his lifeline, though flailing
to save himself, he knocked the glasses
from his head. Now they'd reach the sea
long before him, if he ever would.
He knelt down in the ferns, exhausted,
by fits growing determined never
to leave that spot. They'd find his bones
fifty years from now, clothes and ID

rotted away, a trillium poking through
his ribcage, a cucumber vine trellised
by the seven sockets in his skull.
The play of the thin, unending drizzle
on the overlapping leaves he sank below,
on the bark of the impassive trees
looming around him, grew indistinguishable
from the pulse turning loud in his head.
The ugly bruise on his forehead throbbed.
There were rents and gashes everywhere
down the length of his rain gear, which
let the mist and the dampness in.
Beyond a scant dozen inches, the world
looked blurry, smeared bright, unattainable.
Nothing in his life, up until then
(and if this had been pointed out to him
he would have acknowledged pride in it),
suggested that anything resembling
a speculative turn of mind cannibalized
the adequate, rhythmic, progressive
movements of his thoughts and feelings.
But, still, as almost everyone does,
he'd occasionally had inklings, stirrings,
promptings, and strange intuitions
about something just beyond the radius
of his life—not divine, necessarily,
but what people meant when they referred
to such things—which gave to the least
of his actions its dream of complicity.
Now he recognized, with a shock
almost physical, that those inklings
were just the returning, reanimated echo
(on a different scale but similar
to the echo we sometimes hear in our skulls
which leads us to the uncanny feeling
that an experience we're having is one
we've had before, at some other time—
but does anything ever repeat itself?)
of the vibrations his life made
bouncing off the things around him

sunk deep in their own being;
and that life, his life, blossoming now
in this daisy chain of accident and error,
was nothing more or less than what there was.
There was nothing hidden underneath this,
but it was small, so small, as the life
of his family was, his people, his species
among the other species—firs, owls,
plants whose names he didn't know—
all of them minute, and the earth itself,
its four billion plus years of life
just the faint, phosphorescent track
of a minute sea creature on an ocean
for the annihilating dimensions of which
words such as "infinite" and "eternal"
were ridiculous in their inadequacy.
He lay on his back inside the ferns
and listened to the rain's clepsydral ticking.
He tried to grasp—what was it?—
but it clattered away, that slight change
in the pressure binding thing to thing,
as when an upright sleeper shifts
just a little, imparting to his dreams
an entirely different train of meaning.
Beyond those clouds, the blue was there
which shaded to blackness, and beyond
that blackness the uncounted, terrifying
celestial entities hung suspended only
by the influence they had on one another.
And all of this was just a seed
inside a seed inside a seed. . . .
So that when, finally, late the next morning
he half-crawled out of the woods, and came
in time to a wire fence in a clearing,
less than two feet high and decorated
with gleaming ceramic insulators,
which indicated that a mild current,
five volts at the most, ran through it
to keep the foraging animals off
the newly sown vegetable garden

enclosed inside its perimeter, and saw
beyond it the sprawl of the lawn,
the 4-by-4 parked in the driveway,
the Stars and Stripes on the flagpole,
and the house, he stopped paralyzed.
The wind was blowing northwest, the clouds
were breaking up under its steady persuasion,
but, try as he did, he couldn't will
himself to step lightly over that wire,
and cross the garden's sweet geometry,
and go up to the door and ask to be
fed and made warm and taken home.
By that small fence, he sat down and wept.

from *The Paris Review*

Katyn Forest

◊　◊　◊

I am 1939 and cold air.
I want a cigarette but will make do
with this shovel. This shovel
feels good after stale bread and weeks
in the dark.
To have purpose satisfies.

I am 1939 and too young to smoke.
Don't be absurd.
Joseph Stalin came to dinner and refused
to eat the soup. I have shovel and purpose.
My hands are free only because I do not resist.
I don't scream through sawdust simply because I don't scream.

I am the beginning of a stamp collection:
ten, meticulously affixed to a small card.
I'll be found in a breast pocket, yellowed and peeling.
This place is called Kosygori or Goat Hill.
There are rumors of orchards in the air.
All I ask, really, is that someone forward
our correspondence.

It is 1939 and we are tired.
There is much to be done, but patience
is all we can give. For now I'm content to lie
on the twenty one thousand eight hundred fifty six backs

of my father, press my mouth to the bullet hole
at the base of his skull and hum softly
until my own drum sounds.

from *Another Chicago Magazine*

The Something

◇   ◇   ◇

Here come my night thoughts
On crutches,
Returning from studying the heavens.
What they thought about
Stayed the same,
Stayed immense and incomprehensible.

My mother and father smile at each other
Knowingly above the mantel.
The cat sleeps on, the dog
Growls in his sleep.
The stove is cold and so is the bed.

Now there are only these crutches
To contend with.
Go ahead and laugh, while I raise one
With difficulty,
Swaying on the front porch,
While pointing at something
In the gray distance.

You see nothing, eh?
Neither do I, Mr. Milkman.

I better hit you once or twice over the head
With this fine old prop,
So you don't go off muttering

I saw *something!*

from *The New Yorker*

Beds

◊   ◊   ◊

Terrible beds, soft beds, wily, elusive beds,
beds of half-grown boys, fey and trembling,
dumped on their ear beds of traveling salesmen surprised,
girl beds, and virginal young woman beds,
matronal expansively expressed beds, I think of these,
recalled to sleep, out of sleep into sleep,
waked early, waked late at night remembering,
drunken beds, sopping watery beds, pissed-in beds,
beds come to me, all I have slept in,
beds I have knelt beside and dreamed of,
bench one foot wide for a bed in Saipan,
hay barn in Turkey bed, dawn like sherbert
naked men stood up out of, trickling weedy beds,
greetings and good-byes from beds,
sullen, imperious beds . . . there was always a bed,
place to lie down, if only for a pause, in jail
or in the aisle of a bus, berths below decks
diesel smoke and topside typhoon,
Pacific swells, trough and deepsix beds for lost sailors,
mountain beds often cold and wet,
sooty nights risen from bed drunk
whirling in the yard lie abed in grass
or among tomato vines and springy corn
love gone from my bed
love lost to another's, searching the cold
fabrications for clues, bedstains
and scented sheets, beds of humiliation
and scorn, shivering clothed in unheat until dawn
friend appearing through white cloud said

Go now to the neighbors . . . hot bath like a bed,
and beds of fern and moss
and pine boughs, beds in Istanbul Hotel plush
and beds in Florence and golden Madrid,
Southern beds and beds in New England tucked under quilts,
cornfed beds and *lit de cassis,*
and narrow bed of devotion,
bed of love, of endurance,
bed of turmoil and surrender and change
slow to come, bed of low spoken phrases,
bed of form become style
bed of California grape arbors
and outdoor beds and beds on porches
and beds in back bedrooms where the crazy son died
beds in attics and in upper stories down long stone corridors
beds that trembled and bunk beds
and beds without meaning
beds in trees,
in grass, in fields of clover
beds in fragrant lover's arms,
beds multiplied into
nights sleepless and disordered in beds,
into nights of confusion and dismay,
of lust
of hatred and pride mixed in a sour beam
of persistence, nights of fear,
nights of memory
and applicable recall,
nights of kisses, nights of frankness
passing for truth, nights of delightful smells,
nights on the river, by the sea, inland nights
spoken of in hushed voices, nights by the wayside,
nights come to bed late for no reason,
nights spent for a time sitting on the bathroom floor,
nights and days and the next night in bed
recovering from serious illness, in beds without exits,
beds stepped boldy up to, beds
unfolding like mysteries, childhood beds,
the beds of adulthood and youth,
Chinese beds, decent Norwegian beds,

Filipino tropical beds,
stained beds, beds soaked in perfume, striped
and checkered beds, all night spent
beside someone's bed, beside beds of loved ones,
the bed my father died in burned the next day
in a pit behind the house, my mother's bed empty
for years, beds of my wives, beds of children
raised from their beds and sent forth into the world,
soft and ample and undivided beds, nights lingering
quietly in the mind, beds you spoke of as we lay
after supper calm in our bed, listening to night
come down around us, settled and consonant, happy in our bed . . .

from *Poetry*

Evening's End

◇   ◇   ◇

1943–1970

For the first time in what must be
the better part of two years now
I happened to hear Janis
in her glory—
all that tinctured syrup
dripping off
a razorblade—
on the radio today singing "Summertime."

And it took me back to this girl I knew,
a woman really, my first year
writing undergraduate poetry
at the Mirabeau B. Lamar
State College of Technology
in Beaumont, Texas,
back in 1966.

This woman was the latest in a line,
the latest steady
of my friend John Coyle that spring—
and I remember she was plain:
she was short: and plain
and wore her brown hair up
in a sort of bun in back
that made her plainer still.

I don't know where John met her,
but word went round
she had moved back in with Mom and Dad
down in Port Arthur
to get her head straight,
to attend Lamar,
to study History,
after several years in San Francisco
where she had drifted
into a "bad scene"
taking heroin.

I was twenty,
still lived with Mom and Dad myself,
and so knew nothing
about "bad scenes,"
but I do remember once or twice
each month that spring
John would give a party
with this woman always there.
And always as the evening's end came on
this woman, silent for hours,
would reveal, from thin air,
her guitar,
settle in a chair,
release her long hair
from the bun it was in,
and begin.

Her hair flowed over her shoulders,
and the ends of the strands of hair
like tarnished brass in lamplight
would brush and drag across
the sides of the guitar
as this woman bent
over it.

How low and guttural, how
slow and torchlit, how
amber her song, how absolutely

unlike the tiny nondescript
a few minutes before.—

And I remember also,
from later on that spring,
from May of that year,
two nights in particular.

The first night was a party
this woman gave
at her parents' home.
Her parents' home
was beige:
the bricks the parents' home
was built with
were beige.
The entire house was carpeted
in beige.

John's girl greeted everyone at the door,
a martini in one hand
and a lit cigarette
in an Oriental
ivory cigarette holder in the other,
laughing
for once, and tossing back
her long brown hair.

All the women wore
black full-length party dresses—
and I remember the young woman's father,
how odd he seemed
in his charcoal suit and tie,
his gray hair—
how unamused.

Then John Coyle was drunk.
He spilled his beer
across the beige front room carpet:
that darker dampness sinking in,

the father vanished
from the scene.

The next week we double-dated.
I convinced John and his girl
to see a double feature,
Irma La Douce and *Tom Jones,*
at the Pines Theater.

And I can recall John's girl
saying just one thing that night.

After the films, John was quizzical,
contentious, full of ridicule
for movies I had guaranteed he would enjoy.
He turned and asked her
what she thought—
and in the softest
of tones, a vague rumor
of honeysuckle in the air,
she almost whispered,
"I thought they were beautiful."

That was the last time that I saw her,
the last thing that I heard her say.

A few weeks later,
she drove over to John's house
in the middle of the afternoon,
and caught him in bed
with Suzanne Morain,
a graduate assistant
from the English Department at Lamar.

John told me later
that when she saw them in the bedroom
she ran into the kitchen,
picked up a broom,
and began to sweep the floor—
weeping.

When John sauntered in
she threw the broom at him,
ran out the door,
got in her car and drove away.
And from that day on,
no one ever saw that woman
in Beaumont again.

The next day she moved to Austin.
And later on, I heard,
back to San Francisco.
And I remember when John told me this,
with a semi-shocked expression
on his face, he turned
and looked up, and said, "You know,
I guess she must have really *loved* me."

I was twenty years old.
What did I know?
What could I say?

I could not think
of anything to say,
except, "Yes,
I guess so."

It was summertime.

Thus runs the world away.

from *The Kenyon Review*

MARK STRAND

Morning, Noon and Night

◊　◊　◊

I

And the morning green, and the build-up of weather, and my brows
Have not been brushed, and never will be, by the breezes of divinity.
That much is clear, at least to me, but yesterday I noticed
Something floating in and out of clouds, something like a bird,
But also like a man, black-suited, with his arms outspread.
And I thought this could be a sign that I've been wrong. Then I woke,
And on my bed the shadow of the future fell, and on the liquid ruins
Of the sea outside, and on the shells of buildings at the water's edge.
A rapid overcast blew in, bending trees and flattening fields. I stayed in bed,
Hoping it would pass. What might have been still waited for its chance.

II

Whatever the starcharts told us to watch for or the maps
Said we would find, nothing prepared us for what we discovered.
We toiled in the shadowless depths of noon,
While an alien wind slept in the branches, and dead leaves
Turned to dust in the streets. Cities of light, long summers
Of leisure were not to be ours; for to come as we had, long after
It mattered, to live among the tombs, as great as they are,
Was to be no nearer the end, no farther from where we began.

III

These nights of pinks and purples vanishing, of freakish heat
Stroking our skin until we fall asleep and stray to places
We hoped would always be beyond our reach—the deeps
Where nothing flourishes, where everything that happens seems
To be for keeps. We sweat, and plead to be released
Into the coming day on time, and panic at the thought
Of never getting there and being forced to drift forgotten
On a midnight sea where every thousand years a ship is sighted, or a swan,
Or a drowned swimmer whose imagination has outlived his fate, and who
      swims
To prove, to no one in particular, how false his life had been.

from *The Times Literary Supplement*

JACK TURNER

The Plan

◇　◇　◇

These just-ripe, perfectly packaged blackberries—
    bought at the supermarket yesterday—I had
thought would remind me pleasantly of Grandpa
    and his zinc-colored pails of fresh-picked berries
and his long, black rubber wading boots—worn to ward
    off the briars in the huge, green blackberry field
that now is just a normal-sized parking lot
    with grease spots and cracked, fading-yellow lines.

But these nubbly berries are not perfect. Some of them
    are bitter, some too soft, some too hard—
picked, I guess, by some half-starved Guatemalan
    just trying to make it through the damn day—
not thinking of the pie his wife would soon bake
    or the fresh fish he'd soon fry to eat for supper.
Then again, who cares about blackberries anyway?
    Not me. I'll eat them and go to bed and not care.

At least that's the plan.

from *Poetry*

Infernal

◇ ◇ ◇

Is it better to die by the hand of an intimate
or to die by the hand of a stranger?

The one with his pitchfork and the one with a wing of sorrow
and the one with a shaky plow.

The revenant sprawls by the pool
assessing opulent stucco and glossy indigo.

Planning new calamities for sad girls at the beach house,
their tan lines a testament to self-invention.

It is Miami in the world and in the mind,
the antique candy-striped umbrellas give no protection.

The tourists on Biscayne Boulevard
brandish cameras between pink and green hotels.

On the jetty, in spectral sunlight, in view of lovers, a pelican
swallows heart-shaped fishes one by one.

The time her lover hit her and she ran crying to the door
he said don't run out in the dark, he said I'll drive you.

In traffic the shunt and pull
of engines, exhaust like cirrus scudding earth only lighter.

Where the freeway leaps impossibly skyward
like an inexpressible sentiment (I miss you).

—Packing to ship to the grandkids back east
six varieties of citrus.

The revenant as though he kept secrets
behind sunglasses takes the amnesiac waters.

Sun, triumphant, muscled between clouds,
heat for a moment the nearness we weep for.

I stay close to the water,
you stay close to the shore.

from *Chelsea*

DEREK WALCOTT

Italian Eclogues

◊ ◊ ◊

for Joseph Brodsky

I

On the bright road to Rome, beyond Mantua,
there were reeds of rice, and I heard, in the wind's elation,
the brown dogs of Latin panting alongside the car,
their shadows sliding on the verge in smooth translation,
past fields fenced by poplars, stone farms in character,
nouns from a schoolboy's text, Vergilian, Horatian,
phrases from Ovid passing in a green blur
heading towards perspectives of noseless busts
open-mouthed ruins and roofless corridors
of Caesars whose second mantle is now the dust's,
and this voice that rustles out of the reeds is yours.
To every line there is a time and a season.
You refreshed forms and stanzas, these cropped fields are
your stubble grating my cheeks with departure,
grey irises, your corn-wisps of hair blowing away,
say you haven't vanished, you're still in Italy.
Yeah. Very still. God. Still as the turning fields
of Lombardy, still as the white wastes of that prison
like pages erased by a regime. Though his landscape heals
the exile you shared with Naso, poetry is still treason
because it is truth. Your poplars spin in the sun.

II

Whir of a pigeon's wings outside a wooden window,
the flutter of a fresh soul discarding the exhausted heart.
Sun touches the bell-towers. Clangour of the *cinquecento*,
at wave-slapped landings *vaporettos* warp and depart
leaving the traveller's shadow on the swaying stage
who looks at the glints of water that his ferry makes
like a comb through blonde hair that plaits after its passage,
or book covers enclosing the foam of their final page,
or whatever the whiteness that blinds me with its flakes
erasing pines and conifers. Joseph, why am I writing this
when you cannot read it? The windows of a book spine open
on a courtyard where every cupola is a practice
for your soul encircling the coined water of Venice
like a slate pigeon and the light hurts like rain.
Sunday. The bells of the campaniles' deranged tolling
for you who felt this stone-laced city healed our sins
like the lion whose iron paw keeps our orb from rolling
under guardian wings. Craft with the necks of violins
and girls with the necks of gondolas were your province.
How ordained, on your birthday, to talk of you to Venice.
These days, in book stores I drift towards Biography,
my hand gliding over names with a pigeon's opening claws.
The cupolas enclose their parentheses over the sea
beyond the lagoon. Off the ferry, your shade turns the corners
of a book, and stands at the end of perspective, waiting for me.

III

In this landscape of vines and hills you carried a theme
that travels across your raked stanzas, sweating the grapes
and blurring their provinces: the slow Northern anthem
of fog, the country without borders, clouds whose shapes
change angrily when we begin to associate them
with substantial echoes, holes where eternity gapes
in a small blue door. All solid things await them,
the tree into kindling, the kindling to hearth-smoke,
the dove in the echo of its flight, the rhyme its echo,

the horizon's hyphen that fades, the twigs' handiwork
on a blank page and what smothers their cyrillics: snow,
the white field that a raven crosses with its black caw,
they are a distant geography and not only now,
you were always in them, the fog whose pliant paw
obscures the globe; you were always happier
with the cold and uncertain edges, not blinding sunlight
on water, in this ferry sidling up to the pier
when a traveller puts out the last spark of a cigarette
under his heel, and whose loved face will disappear
into a coin that the fog's fingers rub together.

IV

The foam out on the sparkling strait muttering Montale
in grey salt, a slate sea, and beyond it flecked lilac
and indigo hills, then the sight of cactus in Italy
and palms, names glittering on the edge of the Adriatic.
Your echo comes between the rocks, chuckling in fissures
when the exploding surf subsides, and these lines are a net
for racing sprats, or a catch of rainbow fishes,
the scarlet snapper, the parrot fish, argentine mullet
and the universal rank smell of poetry, cobalt sea
and self-surprised palms at the airport, I smell it,
weeds like hair swaying in water, mica in Sicily,
a smell older and fresher than the Norman cathedrals,
or restored aqueducts, the raw hands of fishermen
their anchor of dialect, and phrases drying on walls
based in moss. These are its origins, verse, they remain
with the repeated lines of waves and their crests, oars
and scansion, flocks and one horizon, boats with keels
wedged into sand, your own island or Quasimodo's
or Montale's lines wriggling like a basket of eels,
I am going down to the shallow edge to begin again,
Joseph, with a first line, with an old net, the same expedition,
I will study the opening horizon, the scansion's strokes of the rain,
to dissolve in a fiction greater than our lives, the sea, the sun.

V

My colonnade of cedars between whose arches the ocean
drones the pages of its missal, each trunk a letter
embroidered like a breviary with fruits and vines,
down which I continue to hear an echoing architecture
of stanzas with St. Petersburg's profile, the lines
of an amplified cantor, his tonsured devotion.
Prose is the squire of conduct, poetry the knight
who leans into the flaming dragon with a pen's lance,
is almost unhorsed like a picador, but tilts straight
in the saddle. Crouched over paper with the same stance,
a cloud in its conduct repeats your hair-thinning shape.
A conduct whose metre and poise were modelled on Wystan's,
a poetry whose profile was Roman and open, the bust
of a minor Caesar preferring a province of distance
to the roar of arenas, a duty obscured by dust.
I am lifted above the surf's missal, the columned cedars
to look down on my digit of sorrow, your stone, I have drifted
over books of cemeteries to the Atlantic where shores
shrivel, I am an eagle bearing you towards Russia,
holding in my claws the acorn of your heart that restores
you past the Black Sea of Publius Naso
to the roots of a beech-tree, I am lifted with grief and praise, so
that your speck widens with elation, a dot that soars.

VI

Now evening after evening after evening,
August will rustle from the conifers, an orange light
will seep through the stones of the causeway, shadows
lie parallel as oars across the long hull of asphalt,
the heads of burnished horses shake in parched meadows
and prose hesitates on the verge of metre. The vault
increases, its ceiling crossed by bats or swallows,
the heart climbs lilac hills in the light's declension,
and grace dims the eyes of a man nearing his own house.
The trees close their doors, and the surf demands attention.
Evening is an engraving, a silhouette's medallion

darkens loved ones in their profile, like yours
whose poetry transforms reader into poet. The lion
of the headland darkens like St. Mark's, metaphors
breed and flit in the cave of the mind, and one hears
in the waves' incantation and the August conifers,
and reads the ornate cyrillics of gesturing fronds
as the silent council of cumuli begins convening
over an Atlantic whose light is as calm as a pond's
and lamps bud like fruit in the village, above roofs, and the hive
of constellations appears, evening after evening,
your voice, through the dark reeds of lines that shine with life.

from *The New York Review of Books*

Diversion

◇ ◇ ◇

Go, I say to myself, tired of my notebooks and my reluctant pen,
go water the newly transplanted sorrel and dill,
spriggy yet in their new humus and larger clay pots;
water artemisia, salvia, centaurea
which are classical, perennial, and have promised to spread their nimbus
of violet and silver through our patchy backyard
for summers to come, from poor soil.
Then I'll return indoors to the words copied
on the yellow legal pad,

her words
    which I cannot shape,
        which sentence me:

"There are things I prefer
to forget—"
    (what things?) "Just,

things—" "Darling, I can't
    locate myself—" "Where
        are *you?*"

and if she, in her compassion, forgets
or doesn't know, I will perennially remember,
how I erase these messages
I later transcribe: one punch
of one button on the answering machine—

and how, with cruel

helpfulness
I have asked:

"Don't you remember?"

restoring to her a garden of incident
which she cannot keep, water, or tend,
and which will die, soon, from her ministrations.

from *The New Republic*

LEWIS WARSH

Downward Mobility

◇　◇　◇

The convict held his breath in the shadow of the doorway as the woman he was following turned her key in the lock. This is where the mystery begins: returning to the scene of the crime, saying this man is a product of my imagination, not myself. He followed her up the steps and wedged his foot in the door of her apartment or entered the apartment through a window and hid behind the curtains. If you're writing about this person it must be you—your fantasy lurking in the shadows, beyond the power of description, beyond the nameless particles of atoms and molecules, the random drops of moisture, the dew on the grass. I stepped out before dawn, at a time when most people are returning from their all night jobs, and put my feet on the grass. Most people think that not to act is a sign of weakness, but sometimes to do something for the sake of doing it is worse. When you don't do anything, people think you don't care. You have to do something to convey how you feel and acting decisively is often the best way. Killing someone who you imagine is the source of your pain is almost everyone's favorite method. What I like to do is call up all my friends, people I haven't seen in years, reserve a booth in an expensive restaurant and order the most expensive items on the menu, flirt with the waitresses, and not eat anything. We seem to be making some progress, an inch or two up the mountain every few weeks. Cordial relations. Simple acts of *politesse*. Considering someone else's point of view, as opposed to thinking only of yourself. I'll probably make the same mistake at least one more time in my life before I learn that there's an alternative. That *I'm* the alternative and that everyone else is cast in doubt. Would you pass the glitter?

from *The World*

Shadow Grammar

◊　◊　◊

If there were a road to the horizon,
if the surface of the water were a staircase
to the rising sun, if I could stand in
the breeze and balance two feathers
on a saxophone, then I would come into the dark
bedroom and lie down with you. We would sing
together and fall asleep and have nightmares
about real estate agents.

Let me tell you about the farm houses
of my past. They stood upon a hill
overlooking a slum. Every day more
animals were born and we gave them names:
Jocopone, Oswald, Florence, Leo. Good
animal names. We loved it there.
We were happy.

But we had to sell, because the market
grew ominous, and move away. We traveled
to this spot to watch the smokestacks
along the shoreline. There is a war
going on between fundamentalists
and drug lords. I hate it, but still
I lie on the beach and sleep with barbarians,
who are everywhere here. There is no escape

for me. My glass is empty. The clocks
stopped ticking long ago. When I'm drunk
I look for interesting rocks along the shore.

from *The World*

EVE WOOD

Recognition

◇ ◇ ◇

The woman on the subway touches my hand by mistake, and in that instant an autumn leaf presses flat against the wet window of the car. She is paler than a snow ferret, and I can see in her face the gentle eagerness of a woman admired all her life solely for her beauty. The leaf inches up the glass, and I feel the heat in her legs radiate out from her body which bumps against mine each time the train lunges forward. I would be so proud if she were my mother, small, blond token of my life, surely an example to follow, yet her mothering would not be enough to keep me. I would want more than is right. Rain leaks in through a crack in the window, and I wish she would look me in the face like the woman who trains dogs on television, who locks the red Doberman's snout between her thumb and forefinger, commanding his attention. I imagine she believes in ghosts and inexplicable passion, and I can do nothing but gnaw the inside of my lip to keep from moving closer. She could start a conversation. She could give herself over. We could hold hands in the rain and not care. The trees blur by, and the mist holds the windows together like a wide gray blanket we might lie down on in summer. Her yellow raincoat hurts my eyes as she leans against me in the wake of the train. She wears me out, and I am still so far from knowing anything.

from *Santa Monica Review*

Disjecta Membra

◊   ◊   ◊

1.

Backyard, dry flower half-border, unpeopled landscape
Stripped of embellishment and anecdotal concern:
A mirror of personality,
                             unworldly and self-effacing,
The onlooker sees himself in,
                                  a monk among the oak trees . . .
How silly, the way we place ourselves—the struck postures,
The soothing words, the sleights-of-hand
                                            to hoodwink the Paraclete—
For our regard; how always the objects we draw out
To show ourselves to effect
(The chiaroscuro of character we yearn for)
Find us a shade untrue and a shade untied.
                             Bad looking glass, bad things.

★

Simplify, Shaker down, the voice drones.
Out of the aether, disembodied and discontent,
No doubt who *that* is . . .
                             Autumn prehensile from day one,
Equinox pushing through like a cold front from the west,
Drizzle and dropped clouds, wired wind.
It's Sunday again, brief devotions.
We look down, dead leaves and dead grass like a starry sky
From inside out.
                             Simplify, open the emptiness, divest—

The trees do, each year milking their veins
Down, letting the darkness drip in,

                          I.V. from the infinite.

    ★

Filing my nails in the Buddha yard.
Ten feet behind my back, like slow, unsteady water,
Backwash of traffic spikes and falls off,
Zendo half-hunched through the giant privet,

                                shut sure as a shell.
Last cat's-eyes of dew crystal and gold as morning fills the grass.
Between Buddha-stare and potting shed,
Indian file of ants. Robin's abrupt arrival
And dust-down.

                Everything's one with everything else now,
Wind leaf-lifter and tuck-in,
Light giving over to shadow and shadow to light.

    ★

I hope for a second chance where the white clouds are born,
Where the maple trees turn red,

                      redder by half than where
The flowers turned red in spring.
Acolyte at the altar of wind,
I love the idleness of the pine tree,

                      the bright steps into the sky.
I've always wanted to lie there, as though under earth,
Blood drops like sapphires, the dark stations ahead of me
Like postal stops on a deep journey.
I long for that solitude,

              that rest,
The bed-down and rearrangement of all the heart's threads.

    ★

What nurtures us denatures us and will strip us down.
Zen says, stand by the side of your thoughts
As you might stand by the bank of a wide river.

                                        Dew-burdened,
Spider webs spin like little galaxies in the juniper bush,
Morning sunlight corpus delicti
                              sprawled on the damp pavement.
Denatures us to a nub.
And sends us twisting out of our backyards into history.
As though by a wide river,
                              water hustling our wants away,
And what we're given, and what we hope to be absolved of . . .
How simply it moves, how silently.

        ★

Death's still the secret of life,
                              the garden reminds us.
Or vice-versa. It's complicated.
Unlike the weed-surge and blossom-surge of early fall,
Unlike the insect husks in the spider's tracery,
Crickets and rogue crows gearing up for afternoon sing-along.
The cottontail hides
                      out in the open, hunched under the apple tree
Between the guillotine of sunlight and guillotine of shade
Beyond my neighbor's hedge.
                              The blades rise and the blades fall,
But rabbit sits tight. Smart bun.
Sit tight and hold on. Sit tight. Hold on.

        ★

Love is more talked about than surrendered to. Lie low,
Meng Chiao advises—
                      beauty too close will ruin your life.
Like the south wind, it's better to roam without design.
A lifetime's a solitary thread, we all learn,
                              and needs its knot tied.
Under the arborvitae,
The squirrels have buried their winter dreams,
                      and ghosts gather, close to home.
My shadow sticks to the trees' shadow.

There is no simile for this,
                    this black into black.
Or if there is, it's my pen point's drop of ink slurred to a word.
Of both, there soon will be not a trace.

★

With what words, with what silence—
Silence becoming speechlessness,
                              words being nothing at all—
Can we address a blade of grass, the immensity of a snowflake?
How is it that we presume so much?
                              There are times, Lord, there are times . . .
We must bite hard into the 21st century,
We must make it bleed.
October approaches the maple trees with its laying on of hands,
Red stains in the appled west,
                              red blush beginning to seep through
Just north of north, arterial headway, cloud on cloud.
Let it come, Lord, let it come.

2.

If I could slide into a deep sleep,
I could say—to myself, without speaking—why my words embarrass me.

Nothing regenerates us, or shapes us again from the dust.
Nothing whispers our name in the night.
Still must we praise you, nothing,
                              still must we call to you.
Our sin is a lack of transparency.

November is dark and doom-dangled,
                              fitful bone light
And suppuration, worn wrack
In the trees, dog rot and dead leaves, watch where you're going . . .

Illegibility. Dumb fingers from a far hand.

★

When death completes the number of the body, its food
Is weeping and much groaning,
                                        and stranglers come, who roll
Souls down on the dirt . . .
                            And thus it is written, and thus believed,
Though others have found it otherwise.

The restoration of the nature of the ones who are good
Takes place in a time that never had a beginning.

Well, yes, no doubt about that.
One comes to rest in whatever is at rest, and eats
The food he has hungered for.
The light that shines forth there, on that body, does not sink.

★

This earth is a handful of sleep, eyes open, eyes shut,
A handful, just that—

There is an end to things, but not here.
It's where our names are, hanging like flesh from the flame trees.

Still, there are no flame points in the sky—

There are no angels, there is no light
At just that point where one said,
                                        this is where light begins.
It dies out in me.

The word is inscribed in the heart.
                                It is beyond us,
The heart, that changeling, word within word.

★

Compulsive cameo, God's blue breath
So light on the skin, so infinite,

Why do I have to carry you, unutterable?
Why do you shine out,
                            lost penny, unspendable thing,

Irreversible, unappeasable, luminous,
Recoursed on the far side of language?
Tomorrow's our only hiding place,
November its last address—
                          such small griefs, such capture.

Insurmountable comforts.
And still I carry you. And still you continue to shine out.

*

Substance. And absence of all substance.
God's not concerned for anything, and has no desire.

Late at night we feel,
                          insensate, immaculata,
The cold, coercive touch of nothing, whose fingerprints
Adhere like watermarks to the skin—

Late at night, our dark and one refuge.

Life is a sore gain, no word, no world.
Eternity drips away, inch by inch, inside us,
December blitzing our blind side,
                          white tongued and anxious.

That's it. Something licks us up.

*

December. Blood rolls back to its wound.
God is a scattered part,
                          syllable after syllable, his name asunder.
No first heaven, no second.

Winter sun is a killer,
                          late light bladed horizon-like
Wherever you turn,
                          arteried, membraned, such soft skin.

Prayers afflict us, this world and the next:

Grief's an eclipse, it comes and it goes.
Photographs show that stars are born as easily as we are.

Both without mercy.

Each leads us away, leads us away.

*

Guilt is a form in itself.
                  As in the love of sentences
That guilt resides in, then darkness.
                       It is as certain.
It is as unregenerative. It is as worn.

Everything terminal has hooks in eternity.
Marsh grass, for instance. Foxfire.
Root work and come-betweens,
                  the Lord's welkin and Lord's will,
As some say in these parts not out loud.
In the bare tines of the lemon tree,
Thorns bristle and nubs nudge,
                  limbs in a reverie of lost loads.
This life is our set-aside, our dry spot and shelter.

*

When slant-light crisps up,
                and shatters like broken lime glass
Through the maple trees, in December,
Who cares about anything but weights and absolutes?

Write up, it's bad, write down, it's still bad.
Remember, everyone's no one.

The abyss of time is a white glove—
                    take it off, put it on,
Finger by finger it always fits,
Buttons mother-of-pearl, so snug, such soft surroundings.

Lord of the broken oak branch,
                Lord of the avenues,
Tweak and restartle me, guide my hand.

3.

Whatever it was I had to say,
                        I've said two times, and then a third.
An object for light to land on,
                        I'm one-on-one with the visible
And shadowy overhang.
It's Christmas Eve, and the Pleiades
Burn like high altar host flames
                        scrunched in the new moon sky—
Their earthly, votive counterparts flash and burst in the spruce tree
And Mrs. Fornier's window.
It's 9:10 and I'm walking the dogs down Locust Avenue.
It's a world we've memorized by heart:
Myopic constellations, dog's bark,
                        bleak supplicants, blood of the lamb . . .

*

Unfinished, unable, distracted—
How easily we reproach ourselves for our lives lived badly,
How easily us undo.
Despair is our consolation, sweet word,
                        and late middle age
And objectivity dulled and drear.
Splendor of little fragments.
Rilke knew one or two things about shame and unhappiness
And how we waste time and worse.
I think I'm starting to catch on myself.
                        I think I'm starting to understand
The difference between the adjective and the noun.

*

Dead moth, old metaphysician, cross-backed, Christ's arrowhead, look,
I'll tell you one thing—
Inch by inch, everyday, our lives become less and less.
Obsessive and skinless, we shrink them down.
And here's another—
                        a line of poetry's a line of blood.

A cross on the back is like a short sword in the heart,
December sun in a fadeaway, cloud under cloud
Over the Blue Ridge,
                              just there, just west of Bremo Bluff.
Okay, I'll keep my mouth shut and my eyes fast on the bare limbs of
                                                    the fruit trees
A line in the earth's a life.

                    ★

O well the snow falls and small birds drop out of the sky,
The backyard's a winding sheet—
                              winter in Charlottesville,
Epiphany two days gone,
Nothing at large but Broncos, pick-ups and 4 × 4s.
Even the almost full moon
                              is under a monochrome counterpane
Of dry grey.
                    Eve of St. Agnes and then some, I'd say,
Twenty-three inches and coming down.
The Rev. Doctor Syntax puts finger to forehead on the opposite wall,
Mancini and I still blurred beside him, Mykonos, 1961,
The past a snowstorm the present too.

                    ★

The human position—anxiety's afterlife, still place—
Escapes us.
                    We live in the wind-chill,
The what-if and what-was-not,
The blown and sour dust of just after or just before,
The metaquotidian landscape
                              of soft edge and abyss.
How hard to take the hard day and ease it in our hearts,
Its icicle and snowdrift and
                              its wind that keeps on blowing.
How hard to be as human as snow is, or as true,
So sure of its place and many names.
It holds the white light against its body, it benights our eyes.

*

The poem uncurls me, corrects me and croons my tune,
Its outfit sharp as the pressed horizon.
                                        Excessive and honed,
It grins like a blade,
It hums like a fuse,
                        body of ash, body of fire,
A music my ear would be heir to.
I glimpse it now and then through the black branches of winter trees.
I hear its burn in the still places.
Halfway through January, sky pure, sky not so pure,
World still in tucker and bib.
Might I slipstream its fiery ride,
                        might I mind its smoke.

*

Is *this* the life we long for,
                        to be at ease in the natural world,
Blue rise of Blue Ridge
Indented and absolute through the January oak limbs,
Turkey buzzard at work on road-kill opossum, up
And flapping each time
A car passes and coming back
                        huge and unfolded, a black bed sheet,
Crows fierce but out of focus high up in the ash tree,
Afternoon light from stage left
Low and listless, little birds
Darting soundlessly back and forth, hush, hush?
                        Well, yes, I think so.

*

Take a loose rein and a deep seat,
                        John, my father-in-law, would say
To someone starting out on a long journey, meaning, take it easy,
Relax, let what's taking you take you.
I think of landscape incessantly,
                        mountains and rivers, lost lakes

Where sunsets festoon and override,
The scald of summer wheat fields, light-licked and poppy-smeared.
Sunlight surrounds me and winter birds
                                doodle and peck in the dead grass.
I'm emptied, ready to go. Again
I tell myself what I've told myself for almost thirty years—
Listen to John, do what the clouds do.

from *The American Poetry Review*

DEAN YOUNG

Frottage

◇   ◇   ◇

How goofy and horrible is life. Just
look into the faces of the lovers
as they near their drastic destinations,
the horses lathered and fagged. Just
look at them handling the vase
priced beyond the rational beneath
the sign stating the store's breakage
policy, and what is the rational but
a thing we must always break? I am not
the only one composed of fractious murmurs.
From the point of view of the clouds,
it is all inevitable and dispersed—
they vanish over the lands to reconstitute
over the seas, themselves again
but no longer themselves, what they wanted
they no longer want, daylight fidgets
across the frothy waves. Most days
you can't even rub a piece of charcoal
across paper laid on some rough wood
without a lion appearing, a fish's umbrella
skeleton. Once we believed it told us
something of ourselves. Once we even believed
in the diagnostic power of ants. Upon
the eyelids of the touched and suffering,
they'd exchange their secretive packets
like notes folded smaller than chemicals.
They told us nearly nothing, which
may have been enough now that we know
so much more. From the point of view

of the ant, the entire planet is a dream
quivering beneath an eyelid, and who's to say
the planet isn't. From the point of view
of the sufferer, it seems everything will
be taken from us except the sensation
of being crawled over. I believe everything
will be taken from us. Then given back
when it's no longer what we want. We
are clouds, and terrible things happen
in clouds. The wolf's mouth is full
of strawberries, the morning's a phantom
hum of glories, morning glories.

from *The Gettysburg Review*

CONTRIBUTORS' NOTES AND COMMENTS

AI was born in the southwest in 1947. She has published five books of poetry: *Greed* (Norton, 1993), and *Fate, Sin, Killing Floor*, and *Cruelty* (Houghton Mifflin). She has received a Guggenheim Fellowship. Her first novel, *Black Blood*, is forthcoming from Norton. She teaches at the University of Colorado in Boulder.

Ai writes: "A while back, I was having some financial difficulties. When I told a friend of mine, an art collector in Phoenix, he offered to lend me some money. A few months later, he said if I wrote a poem for him, he'd forgive the debt. He is a Vietnam vet who lost his best friend and fellow Vietnam vet, not in the war, but in a robbery in Phoenix. I decided to make my character a Vietnam vet too. When I gave him the poem, he said, 'I wasn't expecting anything this good.' "

SHERMAN ALEXIE was born in Spokane, Washington, in 1966. A Spokane/Coeur d'Alene Indian, he is the author of ten books, including *Indian Killer*, a novel (Atlantic Monthly Press, 1996), and *The Summer of Black Widows*, a book of poems (Hanging Loose Press, 1996). He appeared on *Granta*'s list of the twenty finest young American novelists. He lives in Seattle.

Alexie writes: "I wrote 'The Exaggeration of Despair' in direct response to a negative review of my novel *Reservation Blues*. The reviewer, a member of my tribe, contended that I exaggerated the level of despair on my reservation and among Indians in general. I obviously disagreed. I wanted to write a poem (using negative language and imagery to create a chant-like quality) that voiced my disagreement. Obviously, my poem cannot completely reproduce the despair and loss in the Indian world. For that matter, I could never write a poem that completely replicated the level of joy and magic in our lives. My poems are an attempt to capture moments, not whole lives or complete worlds."

AGHA SHAHID ALI, a Kashmiri-American, was born in New Delhi in 1949. He is director of the MFA program in creative writing at the University of Massachusetts, Amherst. "Return to Harmony 3" appears in his latest volume of poems, *The Country Without a Post Office* (Norton), which focuses on the uprising in Kashmir. His previous collections include *The Half-Inch Himalayas* (Wesleyan) and *A Nostalgist's Map of America* (Norton). He has received fellowships from the Ingram Merrill and Guggenheim foundations. He has also translated the Urdu poet Faiz Ahmed Faiz; a volume of these translations, *The Rebel's Silhouette,* was published by Peregrine Smith Books in 1991.

Ali writes: " 'Return to Harmony 3' is among my first attempts at the prose poem. While all my earlier work is in open forms, I could never satisfy myself with anything in the way of a prose poem. My latest volume concentrates on traditional forms (the sonnet, pantoum, canzone, sestina, villanelle, terza rima, ghazal). It was while attempting these rather stringent forms that I stumbled on how I could do a prose poem: by bringing to it all the energy I bring to open and traditional forms but by making the sentence (and paragraph) rather than the line (and stanza) the be-all and end-all of my emotion. I had to teach myself to discard the line completely."

A. R. AMMONS was born on a farm outside Whiteville, North Carolina, in 1926. He started writing poetry aboard a U.S. Navy destroyer escort in the South Pacific. He worked briefly as the principal of an elementary school in Cape Hatteras and later managed a biological glass factory in southern New Jersey. Since 1964 he has taught at Cornell University, where he is the Goldwin Smith Professor of Poetry. He was awarded a MacArthur Fellowship in 1981, the year the "genius awards" were introduced. He has also received the Bollingen Prize (for *Sphere,* in 1975), the National Book Critics Circle Award (for *A Coast of Trees,* in 1981), and the National Book Award, twice—for *Collected Poems: 1951–1971* in 1973 and for the book-length poem *Garbage* in 1993. All these titles were published by Norton. Ammons's other books include *Ommateum* (1955), *Tape for the Turn of the Year* (1965), *The Snow Poems* (1977), *Worldly Hopes* (1982), *The Really Short Poems of A. R. Ammons* (1990), and *Brink Road* (1996). He was the guest editor of *The Best American Poetry 1994.* He and his wife live in Ithaca, New York.

Of "Strip," Ammons writes: "I decided to write a poem on a strip of tape so narrow that the chief subject of the (whole) poem would be complaining about how the lines could not be accommodated to so narrow a compass. I realize that this is sort of cute—but in pursuit of a foolish end, I hoped to touch on serious matters of the mind and heart, in passing. This poem is the first number in a longer series of about one hundred fifty pages."

NIN ANDREWS was born in Charlottesville, Virginia, in 1958, the youngest of six children. She attended Hamilton College and received her MFA at Vermont College. She now lives in Poland, Ohio, with her husband and two children. Her first book of short fiction, *The Book of Orgasms*, was published by Asylum Arts in 1994. Her poems have appeared in *The Paris Review, Michigan Quarterly Review, Exquisite Corpse,* and *Chelsea.*

Of "That Cold Summer," Andrews writes: "Often as children, my friends and I used to pretend we had wings. Attaching towels to our backs with safety pins, we'd leap from sofas and chairs, thudding ungracefully on the floor below. I suppose all of us must wish we were a bit more angelic at one time or another, and perhaps that is why angels are such a hallmark item of our time. But what is it these angels represent to us if not the ability to lift off this planet, to escape the pull of gravity? And this, I think, is one of the reasons I write.

"When I started writing 'That Cold Summer' I was trying to imagine the life of an angel, or some divine being. I wondered how such a creature would look upon the world. One assumes, always, that angels and divinities are above humans, that what we need to do as people is to learn to climb some invisible ladder, as Jacob did in his dream. And yet, what if this were not true? Why not suppose the gods and seraphim envy us, and feel trapped in some cold, ethereal world of eternal light, praying only to lose their wings, plummet like stones, and feast upon earthly fruits? What if human limitations and even death actually were great blessings, and not a curse after all? What if an angel could descend for a few weeks? Of course, she would be destined to ascend again and go back to her passionless ways, since it is the nature of wings to lift off and take one back to the sky.

"So I was thinking when I wrote this poem of an angel in the guise of a woman, interrupting a woman's marriage and then flying away when, like Cinderella, her time for fun was up."

L. S. ASEKOFF was born in Boston, Massachusetts, in 1939 and was raised on the grounds of a state mental hospital, where his father was psychiatric director. He read literature and philosophy at Bowdoin

College, Trinity College (Dublin), and Brandeis University. Since the late 1960s he has taught at Brooklyn College, where he is coordinator of the MFA poetry program and a faculty associate of the Wolfe Institute for the Humanities. He was, for a time, an editor of *Fiction* magazine. He was featured on the cover of the May/June 1993 issue of *The American Poetry Review* and has twice received their Jerome Shestack Prize. Orchises Press (Washington, D.C.) has published his first two books: *Dreams of a Work* in 1994 and *North Star* in 1997.

Of "Rounding the Horn," Asekoff writes: "As a life-long member of the Third Synagogue of the Diaspora, I've founded my shaky faith on Kafka's lament: 'What have I in common with Jews? I hardly have anything in common with myself and should be content to stand in a corner quietly breathing.' Poetry for me is a form of supreme attention and quiet breathing—a listening to what is there. Tone, cadence, song without words. The murmuring sea of language. Sometimes, voices come to me, urgent, oblique, echoing off my own. A friend appears one summer night on my doorstep, wild-eyed, a book on instinct in one hand, an apple in another, confessing his doomed love for young boys—as soon as they begin to grow body hair, shave, his passion withers, though his affection for them remains. A decade later, reading Suetonius, *The Twelve Caesars,* I find myself 'taking dictation,' writing down the words of an ironic, worldly-wise Roman patrician of the late Empire to the young barbarian lover who has outgrown him ('After the Deluge'). 'Rounding the Horn' came to me more directly. It is a collage of my experiences and those of others, friends who were 'a week away from the red chip,' who 'nursed bitter milk from barrels at Baileys,' woke to find the statues talking back to them, those who have seen the white horse standing at the gate, drunk to the bottom of 'the darkest dawns.' The poem, in its loose network of references, puns, allusions, continues my forty-year love affair with Ireland and Irish literature. Beneath the largely transparent surface of the narrative, the manic, desperate voice achieves depth and resonance for me, as writer, when I know the secret—*writerly*—history of each line and detail. For instance, a phrase as unexceptional as 'the little grey lady on the subway' summons up an anecdotal origin unknown (and not immediately relevant) to the reader. Once, riding the subway, I saw a prim older woman a few seats down gesticulating rather dramatically and speaking, it seemed, into thin air. She did not look all that troubled, and yet . . . When I rose to leave the car, I saw to my chagrin seated beside her another, smaller, greyer version of herself—friend? sister? mother?—hidden from my view all the time by her companion's body. Stepping on to the platform, I thought, So, that's what separates the sane from the mad—the little grey lady on the subway."

JOHN ASHBERY was born in Rochester, New York, in 1927. He is the author of sixteen books of poetry, including *Can You Hear, Bird* (Farrar, Straus & Giroux, 1995), and a volume of art criticism, *Reported Sightings*. His *Self-Portrait in a Convex Mirror* received the Pulitzer Prize, the National Book Critics Circle Award and the National Book Award. He is now Charles P. Stevenson, Jr., Professor of Languages and Literature at Bard College. He has been named a Guggenheim Fellow and a MacArthur Fellow, and he is a chancellor of the Academy of American Poets. In 1995, he received the Poetry Society of America's Robert Frost Medal, the highest honor awarded by that institution. He was the guest editor of *The Best American Poetry 1988*.

MARIANNE BORUCH was born in Chicago in 1950. Her first two books, both from Wesleyan University Press, are *View from the Gazebo* (1985) and *Descendant* (1989). *Moss Burning* was published by Oberlin College Press in 1993; Oberlin will also publish her next book, *A Stick That Breaks and Breaks*, in 1998. A collection of her essays, *Poetry's Old Air*, appeared in the University of Michigan Press's Poets on Poetry Series in 1994. She teaches in the MFA program at Purdue.

Of "Camouflage," Boruch writes: "I'm not at all sure how this poem arrived, or why. Maybe certain images passed by me and stayed—the camouflage movie at the Nature Center of the local state park, for one. I do love those weird, zoom-lens closeups of some poor, otherwise nondescript bit of bird or insect, a sudden dramatic marking that lies outright and thus allows whatever it is to live in peace. I wonder about such a thing, the calm violence of it, the connection of beauty and threat. Not that these questions got anywhere near the poem as it unfolded, which is a process too mysterious for me to figure. But I see now that various things I've read or thought about over the years about birds, or the human brain, seeped in. Still, the ending surprised me. I never expected the highway, the dark, least of all that angel."

CATHERINE BOWMAN was born in El Paso, Texas, in 1957. She is the author of two collections, *1-800-HOT-RIBS* (1993) and *Rock Farm* (1996), both from Gibbs Smith. Her work was included in the 1989, 1994, and 1995 editions of *The Best American Poetry*. She received a fellowship from the Texas Institute of Letters in 1994. She teaches at Indiana University and reports on poetry for "All Things Considered" on National Public Radio.

Of "No Sorry," Bowman writes: "I'll start out by saying that I do not believe that all of society is murderous. The hands that create instruments of destruction are also the hands that heal, love, and tend the earth. I wrote this poem in the spring of 1994 while living in the Texas Hill Country on two hundres acres in an old adobe cabin that had once been the home of the writer J. Frank Dobie. The first line was given to me by Sam Stoeltje, age five. Sam and his mother, Melissa, had come down to visit me for the weekend. We were sitting on the limestone porch, the best part of the house. Sam was playing, doing something, I don't remember what. But he came up to me and said, 'Cathy, do you have any scissors I could borrow?' Of course everyone has scissors. Or almost everyone. I had left mine at home in New York City where I had been living for the past seven years. 'No, Sam, sorry I don't,' was my response. But there was something about his question. For some reason it made me feel kind of dizzy, time seemed to slow down and fog up, and at the same time everything was really clear. Maybe it was the heat. Anyway, I went into the house and wrote down those words of Sam's, 'Do you have any scissors I could borrow?' I knew I wanted to use that line for a poem. But how? I kept turning the words over and over in my head. Although Sam's question was perfectly innocent, I decided to imagine a different speaker, unnamed, who might have a different motive for asking the question, and another speaker, also unnamed, answering back. I imagined them in my head as neighbors that might borrow a cup of sugar or milk from each other, only I decided to replace the sugar and milk with barbed wire and missiles. I did a little research on weapons. I learned what I probably always knew, that our weapons are basically variations on the stick and the stone— just much more elaborate and deadly.

"The poem is an anti-ode to escalation. The inevitability in the poem—the sense of knowing what's coming next—mirrors the irrationality of nuclear escalation. The 'No Sorry' refrain acts as a musical beat in the poem, the way a drum beat might keep time in a song. The 'No Sorry' speaker seems patient and polite but is not really apologetic. I wrote the poem in one prose block, the form being a tightly woven question-and-answer game. The media present world events to us in such an abstracted disembodied format—I'm thinking of the Gulf War—that it seems like a game sometimes, something unreal. I shaped the poem so that the listing of weapons has a kind of music, a horrible beauty. Although these weapons are terrifying, it becomes a little amusing to hear them named and listed in such an offhand way. Also, some of the names are ironically quite lovely and 'poetic'—e.g., morning star. The first time I read this poem aloud to an audience a few children in the front broke out into side-splitting laughter. They couldn't stop. This added to the weirdness. Also, when I wrote this poem, I was living on the ranch by myself and I don't know how many well-wishing friends and neighbors advised me to invest in a gun. That was strange, even though I had grown up with guns all around. Still we are all vulnerable no matter what we may keep in our private arsenal. Fighting fire with fire has become an absurdity. How do we defend ourselves when what we most love—the smell of new-mown hay or apple blossoms—has become suspect? (According to my research these are the actual odors used to perfume chemical weapons.) In this sense, the poem questions our inheritances. What legacy have our foremothers and forefathers given us? The 'No Sorry' speaker refuses to take part, and yet may be implicated in the fact that the grandfather's bread knife is connected in some way to this whole lethal scheme."

JOSEPH BRODSKY was born in Leningrad in 1940. In 1963, when Soviet Premier Khrushchev began a crackdown on dissidents, the KGB arrested Brodsky and charged him with "decadence and modernism" and "the writing of awful poems." He was sentenced to five years in internal exile, which he spent in the northern village of Norinskaya. He came to the United States in 1972. Influenced by Auden, he began writing poems in English while working with leading American poets (such as Richard Wilbur and Anthony Hecht) on the English translations of his Russian verse. He taught at Mount Holyoke College. In 1987 he was awarded the Nobel Prize in literature. His book of essays, *Less Than One* (Farrar, Straus & Giroux), won the National Book Critics Circle Award in criticism that year. In 1991 he succeeded Mark Strand as U.S. Poet Laureate. He made a number of radical suggestions while holding that office, among them that poetry anthologies should be sold at supermarket checkout counters and should, like Bibles and phone books, be found in every hotel room in the country. "American poetry is this country's greatest patrimony," he said. "It takes a stranger to see some things clearly. This is one of them, and I am that stranger." Despite a history of heart attacks, he smoked with heroic abandon and made gallows humor out of the subject of his own mortality. ("Husband to wife: the doctor says I will die before another daybreak. Let's have champagne and make love one last time. Wife to husband: easy for you—you don't have to get up in the morning.") He died in 1996. "Love Song" appears in his posthumous volume *So Forth* (Farrar, Straus & Giroux).

STEPHANIE BROWN was born in Pasadena, California, in 1961 and grew up in Newport Beach. She has degrees from Boston University, the University of Iowa Writers' Workshop, and the University of California at Berkeley. Her poems were included in the 1993 and 1995 editions of *The Best American Poetry*. Most recently, she was the featured poet of the July/August 1996 issue of *The American Poetry Review*. "Feminine Intuition" is from a manuscript entitled "Fitness." A senior librarian in the collection department of the Orange County public library system, Brown lives in San Clemente with her husband and their two young sons.

Of "Feminine Intuition," Brown writes: "A couple of notes: The three parts of the poem are meant to suggest the three parts (Kore, Demeter, Hecate) of the female life story. 'A Woman Clothed with the Sun' " is another name for the Virgin Mary. The more I try to write about this poem, the more it resists me . . . so I'll leave it at that."

JOSHUA CLOVER was born in Berkeley in 1962. He writes that he "finished next-to-last in my class in high school. I abandoned film school after a semester to work at a bookstore in Manhattan where Thurston Moore used to lean against a shelf reading Philip K. Dick. Deejayed at King Tut's Wah-Wah Hut; was an understudy for the role of Ivan Tchcheglov in *Hacienda!;* my only furniture was a child's desk, red. When I returned to school I changed my name from Kaplan to Clover (ten bucks); deejayed at the 6:20 Club (the only place in eastern Iowa to appear in the *Gay Yellow Pages*). I spent a year at Fine Arts Work Camp; deejayed at WORM, graveyard shift and morning wake-up. A grant from the Copernicus Society ("and yet its doughs move") and then an Any A Fellowship: winter and spring follow in San Cristobal of the Houses, living in hotels; I have a crush on a waitress who swears I work for the CIA. And so on—Trotsky's 'continual revolution' writ small. Or perhaps a miniature 'dustbin of history'—Trotsky again, playboy of the world western. He appears briefly in *Madonna anno domini* (Walt Whitman Award, Academy of American Poets; LSU Press, 1997)."

Of "The Map Room," Clover writes: "This commenting on objects made physically from words with more words is a curious practice— particularly since I think of poems themselves as comments on some metaphysic: immanence, sex, whatever. Notes about poems are like unto poems about *Gravity's Rainbow* (though a haiku with the median line 'Tantivy Mucker-Maffick' would have its own appeal). My poems are always annotations of whatever music I am listening to and vice versa. Like most dates 'The Map Room' starts at the movies and ends in bed; it annotates and is equally annotated by the Matthew Sweet EP 'The Ugly Truth' so perhaps I should refer you there—particularly to 'Ultrasuede' and 'Ugly Truth Rock.'"

BILLY COLLINS was born in New York City in 1941. His recent books include *The Art of Drowning* (University of Pittsburgh Press, 1995) and *Questions About Angels* (William Morrow, 1991), which Edward Hirsch selected for the National Poetry Series. He has won the Bess Hokin Prize, the Frederick Bock Prize, the Oscar Blumenthal Prize, and the Levinson Prize, all awarded by *Poetry* magazine. A recipient of a Guggenheim Fellowship and a grant from the National Endowment for the Arts, he is a professor of English at Lehman College (CUNY). He lives with his wife in northern Westchester County.

Of "Lines Lost Among Trees," Collins writes: "Anyone in the habit of carrying a notebook—keeping a log of the self—knows what it feels like to be caught naked without pen and paper when some pigeon of inspiration lands on your head. 'Lines Lost Among Trees' is about such an experience. The poem is meant to commemorate another poem, a forgotten one, a ghost poem which I still sense lurking somewhere in the background. I wrote it one afternoon after I returned from a walk, bereft of some lines that had come to me while padding around in the woods near our house. As I mulled over the loss, I was moved to begin a kind of light elegy for those lines that had died without the life-support of memory.

"The farewell gesture toward the end of the poem is modeled after the envoy in Chaucer's *Troilus and Criseyde* ('Go, litel book, go myn tragedye'), the poet's good-bye to his own work as it leaves his hands and enters the world, only here, the poem has left my memory and enters the void."

GILLIAN CONOLEY was born in Taylor, Texas, in 1955. Her collections of poetry include *Beckon* (Carnegie Mellon University Press, 1996); *Tall Stranger* (Carnegie Mellon University Press, 1991), *Some Gangster Pain* (Carnegie Mellon University Press, 1987); and *Woman Speaking Inside Film Noir* (Lynx House Press, 1984). *Tall Stranger* was nominated for the National Book Critics Circle Award. She has received awards and fellowships from the Academy of American Poets, the Washington Council for the Arts, and the Coordinating Council of Literary Magazines and Small Presses. She is the founder and editor of *Volt* and teaches at Sonoma State University. She lives with her husband and daughter in Corte Madera, California.

Of "The Sky Drank In," Conoley writes: "I guess the poem is part of an ongoing struggle to represent the shackles of identity and how one must circle around them, slip out from under them, if only momentarily, to be truly alive; I suppose this is a theme one could trace through all of my books. The difficulties of love in our time, of desiring to be *one,* the impossibility of that, are also present in the poem. I remember at the time I wrote this I was reading a lot of feminist criticism, especially Luce Irigaray and Hélène Cixous, and thinking a lot about presence and existence, expectation and projection, identity and multiplicity. The idea of one's projections becoming 'a screen,' a kind of looking-glass, comes directly from Luce Irigaray."

JAYNE CORTEZ was born in Arizona, grew up in California, and currently lives in New York City. She is the author of ten books of poetry and performer on eight recordings of poetry. Her poems have been translated into many languages and published in journals, magazines, and anthologies such as *Daughters of Africa, Women on War, Jazz & Poetry, Free Spirits, Black Scholar, Sulfur,* and *UNESCO Courier.* She has lectured and read her poetry, with and without musical accompaniment, throughout North America, South America, Africa, Asia, Europe, and the Caribbean. Her most recent book is *Somewhere in Advance of Nowhere* (Serpent's Tail/High Risk Books, 1996). With her band, The Firespitters, she has recorded six CDs. Her latest CD, *Taking the Blues Back Home,* was released by Verve/Polygram in 1996.

Cortez writes: "The Museum of Natural History is a fertile place for combinations of reality and the imagination."

ROBERT CREELEY was born in 1926 in Arlington, Massachusetts, in 1926. He is a New Englander by birth and disposition, although he has spent most of his life in other parts of the world, including Guatemala, British Columbia, France, and Spain. In the 1950s he taught at Black Mountain College and also edited the *Black Mountain Review.* Charles Olson, then rector of the college, Robert Duncan, and Edward Dorn are among the company he met there. Subsequently he taught at the

University of New Mexico and in 1966 went to the State University of New York at Buffalo, where he still teaches as the Samuel Capen Professor of Poetry and the Humanities. Although usually identified as a poet (*For Love, Pieces, Windows,* and *Selected Poems* are examples of his many collections), he has written a significant body of prose, including a novel, *The Island,* and a collection of stories, *The Gold Diggers,* all of which can be found in *The Collected Prose of Robert Creeley.* His critical writings are published in *The Collected Essays of Robert Creeley* and his correspondence with Charles Olson is now in ten volumes *(The Complete Correspondence).* He is working with Buffalo's City Honors School to put students online with a journal of their own writing (http://cityhonors.buffalo.k12.ny.us/chs), thanks to a Lila Wallace–Reader's Digest Writers Award.

Of "Won't It Be Fine?" Creeley writes: "This poem, like they say, was written early evening some months ago while listening to James Booker playing and singing the song of the same title. I had the tape thanks to fellow poet Duncan McNaughton, whose notes are to the point: 'Booker b. 1939—d.early 80's. Time in various SW Louisiana bughouses & at Angola, bi-sexual mad-head, I expect the last of the crowd of post-war piano players, tho' I hope not. He knew the whole book. (A little bit of how come I like evenings in New Orleans better than those around here.)' I can dig it."

CARL DENNIS was born in St. Louis in 1930. He now lives in Buffalo, where he teaches at the State University of New York. His seventh book of poems, *Ranking the Wishes,* was published by Penguin in 1997.

Dennis writes: "The germ of 'History' was the reading of a work of history by a writer who had succumbed to the occupational hazard of his profession, the presumption that what has happened is all that could have happened rather than being merely one of many possibilities available at any particular moment."

WILLIAM DICKEY was born in Bellingham, Washington, in 1928, and grew up in the Pacific Northwest. He was educated at Reed College, Harvard University, and the University of Iowa Writers' Workshop. He was later a Fulbright Fellow at Jesus College, Oxford University. He wrote fifteen books of poetry, including *Of the Festivity,* which was chosen by W. H. Auden for the Yale Series of Younger Poets in 1959; *More Under Saturn* (1963); *The Rainbow Grocery* (1978), which won the Juniper Prize; *King of the Golden River* (1986), which won the Bay Area

Book Award; and *In the Dreaming: Selected Poems* (Arkansas, 1994). *The Education of Desire,* his last completed collection of poems, appeared posthumously from Wesleyan University Press in 1996. In the same year, Eastgate Systems, a software publisher in Massachusetts, published *The Complete Electronic Poems of William Dickey* as a two-volume set on diskette and CD-Rom. He died in San Francisco in 1994.

William Dickey had wanted to write a poem about John Berryman, his former teacher at the University of Iowa, for a very long time. Yet he was hesitant, fearful that his skills as a poet were not equal to the admiration, respect, and gratitude he felt for Berryman as a teacher. When the poem arrived in early November 1994, it came nearly complete. Dickey finished the poem on November 29, five months before his own death in San Francisco from HIV-related causes.

ROBERT DOW was born in the Hub. He is a Vietnam veteran.

Of "How Should I Say This?" Dow writes: "The image of the boot was what triggered the piece. I took that image, that idea, as far as I could, but the piece was far from complete and I knew it. Something was missing and I was at a loss as to what to do next. Somehow the question 'how should I say this?' came to mind. I found myself inside the poem where I needed to be. The first-person narrative line got me to the image of the burning drums. Anyway, that's how it seems in hindsight. There were dozens of rewrites. I kept on putting things in and taking things out; that aspect of the writing went on endlessly. I'm sure if I were to look at the poem again I would still fiddle around with it.

"What you need is some luck, some will, some patience."

THOMAS SAYERS ELLIS was born in Washington, D.C., in 1963 and currently resides in Cleveland, Ohio, where he is an assistant professor of English at Case Western Reserve University. A founding member of the Dark Room Collective, he received his MFA at Brown University in 1995 and was a fellow at the Provincetown Fine Arts Work Center in Provincetown, Massachusetts, in 1995–96. His poems have appeared in *AGNI, Boston Review, Callaloo, Grand Street, Harvard Review, Kenyon Review, Southern Review,* and *The Garden Thrives: Twentieth-Century African American Poetry.* His first collection, *The Good Junk,* appeared in the *AGNI* annual *Take Three* (Graywolf, 1996).

Ellis writes: " 'Atomic Bride' is one of a series of poems about and inspired by Parliament/Funkadelic, aka P-Funk. It was triggered by the image of guitarist Andre Foxxe pimping across the stage in a wedding dress; and it samples, clones and riffs on P-Funk's 'If you ain't gonna get it on, take your dead ass home' approach to getting dressed, change, transformation (See *Computer Games,* Capitol Records, 1982). I initially thought of writing it as a villanelle then decided the villanelle was too slow—33 when I needed 45—so I sped it up (the way Funkadelic *sped* the Blues up) by using short tercets—the irony being that threes are the antithesis of The One in P-Funk cosmology. I would like to dedicate this publication to the members of the Dark Room Collective (past and present) who tolerated my P-Funkiness, a positive nuisance; and to Nat of Nat's Record Shop (formerly of 7th & P Streets, N.W., Chocolate City) for groovallegiance needful as gravy, and cutout bins deep as the cosmos. Fly on!"

IRVING FELDMAN was born in Brooklyn, New York, in 1928. He is the author of *New and Selected Poems* (Viking Penguin, 1979), *Teach Me, Dear Sister* (Viking Penguin, 1983), *All of Us Here* (Viking Penguin, 1986), and *The Life and Letters* (University of Chicago Press, 1994). In 1986 he received a grant from the National Endowment for the Arts, and in 1992 he was made a MacArthur Fellow. He is Distinguished Professor of English at the State University of New York at Buffalo.

Feldman writes: " 'Man is an audacity seeking confirmation' (Martin Buber)."

HERMAN FONG was born in Los Angeles in 1963 and grew up in the San Fernando Valley. A recipient of an AWP Intro Award and two Academy of American Poets prizes, he is an MFA candidate at the University of Massachusetts in Amherst. His poems have appeared in the *Gettysburg Review* and *Indiana Review.* He divides his time between southern California and Northampton, Massachusetts.

Of "Asylum," Fong writes: "I began this poem after receiving a letter from a friend. She told me of a woman in her nineties who wrung the heads off of chickens and gutted them with only her own small hands. A short time later, while hiking through woods, I found a tree with a rusted ax head embedded in its thick trunk.

"I have always been interested in exploring how individuals confronted with the calamity and complexities of daily living respond, whether they surrender themselves to sadness and despair."

DICK GALLUP was born in Greenfield, Massachusetts, in 1941. He moved to Tulsa, Oklahoma, in 1950. He attended Tulane University and graduated from Columbia University. His books include *Hinges* (C Press, 1965), *The Bingo* (Mother Press, 1966), *Where I Hang My Hat* (Harper & Row, 1970), *The Wacking of the Fruit Trees* (Toothpaste Press, 1975), *Above the Tree Line* (Big Sky, 1976), and *Plumbing the Depths of Folly* (Smithereens Press, 1983). He received a poetry fellowship from the National Endowment for the Arts in 1979. He has held administrative positions at the Poetry Project at Saint Mark's Church (1972), the Jack Kerouac School of Disembodied Poetics (1977–79), and the Boulder Public Library, Boulder, Colorado (1977–78). He taught extensively in Poetry-in-the-Schools programs between 1969 and 1981. Currently he is driving a taxicab in San Francisco, where he lives.

Of "Backing into the Future," Gallup writes: "Missing the bus can be a terrible experience, reminding you that time goes entirely too fast in the modern world. I suspect it passed too quickly in the ancient world as well. If we could zoom up a level into geologic time, we might see our whole life as the meandering of a microscopic bug on a slide. Yikes! Looking up from the microscope, it's easy to imagine being cast far into the future, which would probably be even more disconcerting.

"In 1965, the poet Ted Berrigan was working on a long poem entitled 'Destination Moon.' It was a very strange work that contained a monkey who sat at a desk with his fingers poised over the space-bar of a typewriter. The monkey somehow ended up on the moon from this quasi-meditative activity. This poem contained a passage in which Ted (not the monkey) found himself deep underground where the doors 'fretted open' and left him with 'no will to go on.' The image has fascinated me all these years, and dislocating it thirty years into the future seemed appropriate. Nonetheless, some kind of consistency of character or nature does exist in our lives. In my own case, a childhood spent on the edge of a small New England town, with pastures, brooks, and second-growth woods out the back door seems to have produced a relationship to nature that has sustained my sense of self through the years.

"Ted never did finish his poem, though he did use the material in other places. It was about the time he was working on his famous 'interview' with John Cage."

MARTIN GALVIN was born in Philadelphia in 1937. He was educated at Villanova University and the University of Maryland. A recently retired teacher—he taught at Walt Whitman High School in Bethesda, Maryland, for twenty-five years—Galvin has published two volumes of poetry. *Wild Card* (Washington Writers' Publishing House) was selected by Howard Nemerov for the Washington Poetry Committee Prize in 1989. *Making Beds* is a hand-sewn and -bound chapbook from Sedwick Press.

Of "Introductions," Galvin writes: "I have a happy, though not always successful, acquaintance with fictional monologue in its various guises and a belief that, in my own poetry, it is a reliable way to free myself from the hobgoblins that dance attendance. 'Introductions' allows some biographical surprises as the character lets parts of his life out—details that the reader will not be surprised to hear that the writer did not know would emerge when he started.

"My father was a railroad man, though in the Great Depression, he did sell one large kitchen appliance—to a relative, as the story goes. I have had the good fortune of spending almost all my conscious life trying to teach words and students to mix, but in one early moment, pushed by a Minor Deflation, I, jobless, managed to sell one set of encyclopedias—to a friend of a relative's friend, as the story continues. The salesman-narrator's problem with forgetting names, however, is a more universal one than bad jokes, I suspect.

"While I do have three brothers, and one of them did serve in Vietnam, we were spared a dying. Like the narrator, I had a childhood I sometimes remember better than I want to, better than when to use *which*, when to use *that*, better than yesterday's big news. So now you have almost all my secrets: putting on masks and accepting surprises. And taking some pleasure in honing tone. I'm glad, too, I got to know the narrator of 'Introductions' a little bit."

AMY GERSTLER was born in 1956 in San Diego, California. She teaches in the graduate fine arts department at Art Center College of Design in Pasadena, California, and has taught in the writing program at the University of California, Irvine. She has written fiction and journalism and has collaborated with choreographers and visual artists. Her eighth book, *Bitter Angel,* published by North Point Press, won the National Book Critics Circle Award in poetry in 1991. A new book, *Crown of Weeds,* will be published by Viking Penguin in 1997.

Of "A Fan Letter," Gerstler writes: "While attempting to write a sincere fan letter to a writer whose work has meant a great deal to me, I ran into an obstacle I was unable to overcome. The problem was that I was so in awe of this person's writing, and my respect for the work was so intense, that no matter how hard I tried not to, I seemed unable to avoid sounding like a fawning, overzealous, possibly annoying, dithering nut. *This will not do,* I thought. *You will only scare this writer, whom you do not know, when your wish is to express gratitude and admiration, not make them feel creepy for the rest of the week. Better not to write to this person at all than to send them a letter which will discomfort them and make them think their fans are, as they used to say, 'head cases.'* Because it's easy for me to slip into feeling a bit demented, and because I often like to write from the point of view of someone in an addled and/or altered psychological state, I decided the best course of action was to abandon the idea of sending any fan letters, and to go ahead and try to make it a poem instead, so I could just feel free to push the battiness to extremes, have a laugh at myself, and play with the idea of the overwrought fan who's projecting all sorts of crazy stuff onto the letter's unlucky recipient."

ALLEN GINSBERG was born in Newark, New Jersey, in 1926. He attended Columbia College, where he studied with Lionel Trilling and Meyer Schapiro; when Ginsberg wrote the words "fuck the Jews" in the dust of his dormitory windowsill, the dean of the college summoned Trilling to his office and, too aghast to utter the words, wrote them on a slip of paper. In *On the Road,* Jack Kerouac based the character of Carlo Marx on Ginsberg. When the poet read "Howl" at San Francisco's North Beach in 1956, he uttered the battle cry of the Beat movement. The poem was banned and became a cause célèbre. Other poems of this period, such as "America" ("America I'm putting my queer shoulder to the wheel") and "Kaddish," his elegy for his mother ("Get married Allen don't take drugs"), were among the most seminal works in the countercultural literary uprisings of the 1960s. In that decade, Ginsberg chanted mantras, sang poems, advocated peace and pot, and fused the influences of William Blake, William Carlos Williams, Eastern mysticism, and Hebrew prophecy in his work. Crowned May King in Prague in 1965, Ginsberg was promptly expelled by Czech police. To a Senate subcommittee investigating the use of LSD in 1966, he said, "if we want to discourage use of LSD for altering our attitudes, we'll have to encourage such changes in our society that nobody will need to take it to break through to common sympathy." Once, at a reading, a heckler shouted, "What do you mean, nakedness?" Ginsberg stripped off his clothes in response. "Under all this self-revealing candor is purity of heart," says the narrator of Saul Bellow's *Him with His Foot in His Mouth.* "And the only living representative of American Transcendentalism is that fat-breasted, bald, bearded homosexual in smeared goggles, innocent in his uncleanness."

Ginsberg traveled to and taught in the People's Republic of China, the former Soviet Union, Scandinavia, and Eastern Europe. His recent books include *Collected Poems 1947–1980* (Harper & Row, 1984), *White Shroud: Poems 1980–1985* (1985), and *Cosmopolitan Greetings: Poems 1986–1992* (HarperCollins, 1994). Several volumes of his photographs have been published, including *Snapshot Poetics* (Chronicle Books, 1993). Ginsberg was diagnosed with liver cancer in April 1997. He died of a heart attack on April 5, 1997.

DANA GIOIA was born in Los Angeles in 1950. He attended Stanford University, studied literature at Harvard, then returned to Stanford where he went to business school. From 1977 through 1992 he worked as an executive at a major corporation headquartered near New York City. He is now a full-time writer. He has published two books of poetry, *Daily Horoscope* (Graywolf, 1986) and *The Gods of Winter* (Graywolf, 1991), as well as a controversial volume of criticism, *Can Poetry Matter?* (Graywolf, 1992). He is currently writing an opera libretto, *Nosferatu,* for the composer Alva Henderson. In 1996 Gioia returned to the West after two decades in New York. He now lives with his wife and children outside Santa Rosa, California.

Gioia writes: "I could say a great many things about 'The Litany,' but most of them would matter far more to the author than to anyone else. The poem will, I suppose, seem difficult to readers eager for the paraphrasable content of workaday prose. I hope the poem is not opaque, but neither did I want the language to be transparent. A reader will either understand 'The Litany' intuitively or not at all. It will help, though, to read the poem aloud. Its organization is musical. Though not all art aspires to the conditions of music, this poem wants to be heard and not seen. What better way than music to describe the invisible?"

ELTON GLASER was born in New Orleans in 1945. A professor of English at the University of Akron, he is the director of the University of Akron Press. Three full-length collections of his poems have been published: *Relics* (Wesleyan University Press, 1984), *Tropical Depressions* (University of Iowa Press, 1988), and *Color Photographs of the Ruins* (University of Pittsburgh Press, 1992). He has received two fellowships from the Ohio Arts Council, the *Louisiana Literature* Poetry Prize and the Ohioana Poetry Award, for his "significant contribution to the poetry of Ohio." "Undead White European Male" appeared in *The Best American Poetry 1995.*

Glaser writes: "W. D. Snodgrass, in one of his essays, concludes that the poet aims at two qualities difficult to achieve, especially in combination: truth to experience and powerful expression. Had Snodgrass put that point in Freudian terms, a dialect with which he was familiar, he might have said that the poet should proceed as if there were no difference between the reality principle and the pleasure principle.

" 'Smoking,' a single long sentence developed mostly by process analysis, has no patience with the Puritan pieties of our time, this frightened and coercive age in which we too often find, as Shakespeare phrased it, 'art made tongue-tied by authority.' But the poem is also alert to the consequences of the sensual. It wants neither to flinch at pleasure nor to flinch from pain.

"The materials for 'Smoking,' luckily, were at hand, and the end came, as it always does, when the poem had exhausted its matter—an end that, however distant from the beginning, is both natural and inevitable. The lines give themselves to the kinship of syllables, to the word unexpected but precise, to image reaching after image until there is nothing left to say. The rest is rhythm, in measures of irregular breath."

KATE GLEASON was born in New Hampshire in 1956. She has two collections of poetry: *Making As If to Sing* (Amherst Writers & Artists Press, 1989) and *The Brighter the Deeper* (winner of the 1995 Embers chapbook contest). Her work has appeared in *Green Mountains Review, Sonora Review, The Spoon River Poetry Review, Midland Review, Room of One's Own, Poets On, The Little Magazine, Sojourner,* the *Anthology of Magazine Verse and Yearbook of American Poetry,* and Beacon Press's *Claiming the Spirit Within.* She studied writing at Amherst Writers & Artists and at the University of Massachusetts. Formerly the editor of *Peregrine* literary journal and a Poet-in-the-Schools, she currently teaches creative writing workshops in the Monadnock region of southern New Hampshire.

Gleason writes: " 'After Fighting for Hours' was the result of trying to write about what it takes to keep a marriage together over the long haul, to go the distance, and how the key to doing that is often of an elemental, illogical, and nonverbal nature, simply letting the dumb animals of our bodies take their course. Originally the poem was titled 'The Wisdom of the Body,' and these fourteen lines made up its final stanza. They were preceded by a stanza of thirty long-winded lines—each beginning with the word 'when . . .'—which listed the escalating and, ultimately, failed attempts of a couple trying to fight their way through a huge rift back to connectedness. Although I liked much of the language in the thirty lines, the two stanzas felt like separate poems. This actually made it an easy piece to revise. I simply cut off its head and then encapsulated the discarded thirty lines in the new title 'After Fighting for Hours.' "

ALBERT GOLDBARTH was born in Chicago in 1948. He currently lives in Wichita, Kansas (although he has lived, as his poem indicates, in Austin, Texas). He is the author of numerous collections of poetry, including *Heaven and Earth: A Cosmology* (University of Georgia Press, 1992), which received the National Book Critics Circle Award, and— his most recent collection—*Adventures in Ancient Egypt* (Ohio State University Press, 1996). *Great Topics of the World* (cloth, David R. Godine; paper, Picador USA/St. Martin's) is the more recent of his two volumes of personal essays.

Goldbarth writes: "Purist? Or curmudgeon? In any case, I prefer that this poem, like all of my poems, stand independent of any after-the-fact commentary. (I'm also drawing the line at mandatory MTV-style videos for all poets. Can't you just feel it coming?)"

JORIE GRAHAM was born in New York City in 1950. She grew up in Italy, studied in French schools, and attended the Sorbonne, New York University, Columbia University, and the University of Iowa. She has published six books of poetry: *Hybrids of Plants and of Ghosts* (1980) and *Erosion* (1983) from Princeton University Press; *The End of Beauty* (1987), *Region of Unlikeness* (1991), *Materialism* (1993), and *The Dream of the Unified Field: Selected Poems 1974–1994* (1995) from the Ecco Press. She has received a MacArthur Fellowship and the Morton Dauwen Zabel Award from the American Academy of Arts and Letters. She lives in Iowa City with her husband and daughter and teaches at the University of Iowa Writers' Workshop. She was the guest editor of *The Best American Poetry 1990*. She received the Pulitzer Prize in poetry in 1996.

DONALD HALL was born in Connecticut in 1928, and in 1942 decided to write poetry for the rest of his life. Afternoons, coming home from a suburban high school, he worked on poems; summers on the farm in New Hampshire, he wrote in the morning. In 1975 Hall and his wife Jane Kenyon moved from Michigan to New Hampshire, where he writes in the room where he wrote in the 1940s. His latest book of poems is *The Old Life* (Houghton Mifflin, 1996). He was the guest editor of *The Best American Poetry 1989*.

Of "The Porcelain Couple," Hall writes: "My wife Jane was diagnosed with leukemia 31 January 1994. Seven weeks later my mother died at ninety, and I had to empty her house in Connecticut. Under ordinary circumstances Jane and I would have spent a week making choices about the disposition of my mother's things—but Jane was too sick, at our house in New Hampshire, and I could not bear to be away from her too long. On 23 April I drove four hours to empty my mother's house, a week before the new family moved in; I drove back the same day.

"People who dismantle parental houses dread the dismantling of their own. Jane's illness exacerbated this dread. The day after my trip I took notes toward this poem, and worked it over during the next twelve months as I sat beside Jane's bed in the hospital or at home. 'The Porcelain Couple' began at four or five times its present length, sunken under detail and circumstance. I wrote about the drive from New Hampshire to Connecticut, and about help from my children and a neighbor. I listed the contents of drawers and closets and tabletops—the multitudinous relics of a long life, bound for the dump like everything and everyone. At one point I listed forty-odd objects or categories of objects; maybe I still list too many, but in revision I omitted the names of most things—as well as mention of my helpers.

"As I worked on this poem during the last year of Jane's life, I read it aloud to her from time to time, and she helped me. Among more important matters, she changed the title. First I had called it 'The Ceramic Couple.' "

DANIEL HALPERN is the author of seven collections of poetry, most recently *Foreign Neon* (Knopf, 1991) and *Selected Poems* (Knopf, 1994), and has received fellowships from the Guggenheim Foundation and the National Endowment for the Arts. He is editor-in-chief of the Ecco Press and was the founder and editor of *Antaeus,* the international literary magazine, which he edited from 1969 to 1995. In 1993, he was awarded the PEN Publisher Citation for his work at Ecco. He has edited numerous anthologies, including *Plays in One Act, Writers on Artists,* and *The Art of the Tale: An International Anthology of Short Stories.* He has taught at the New School for Social Research, Princeton University, and for twenty years in the graduate writing program of Columbia University. He divides his time between New York and Princeton, New Jersey, where he lives with his wife and daughter.

Of "Her Body," Halpern writes: "If you write poetry and have a child later in life, your pals warn you to steer clear of poems that look to describe or celebrate the experience. I resisted through the first year, then succumbed while in Maine watching and listening to our bay's tidal activity practice the elemental—giving over, taking back—reminding me of the ephemeral nature of my relationship to *breath,* which brought me speedily to my daughter Lily, her moment in this summer of her first year, as well as to her future. Or more accurately, my future in her future. And so it happened that I allowed what pursued me day and night access to the page, allowed the cycles of life at the midpoint to carry me forward to this poem. If sentimentality is loving a thing more than god does (Salinger?), I found myself in a deeply sentimental mood. I found myself without warning writing this poem, letting it spill out emotional euphoria derived from witnessing the first year of a daughter. Writing 'Her Body' felt like my second true gift to her, which years from now she might read with understanding and know the ways in which her parents were preoccupied with her presence in our lives. The poem's a scrapbook, a poem of thanks and appreciation—to acknowledge something that goes beyond anything we can say about it."

ROBERT HASS was born in San Francisco in 1941. He teaches at the University of California at Berkeley. His books include *Praise* and *Human Wishes* (Ecco, 1989). He has also co-translated several volumes of the poems of Czeslaw Milosz, including *Provinces* (Ecco, 1991). He was appointed U.S. Poet Laureate in 1995, succeeding Rita Dove. During his stint Hass wrote a weekly column on poetry for *The Washington Post Book World.* His most recent collection, *Sun Under Wood* (Ecco, 1996), received the National Book Critics Circle Award in poetry.

BOB HICOK was born in Michigan in 1960. He is an automotive die designer and computer system administrator and lives in Ann Arbor, Michigan. His books include *The Legend of Light* (University of Wisconsin Press, 1995), which Carolyn Kizer chose as the winner of the Felix Pollak Prize in poetry. An earlier volume is entitled *Bearing Witness* (Ridgeway Press, 1991). His third collection, *Kinship,* will be published by BOA Editions in the fall of 1998.

Of "Heroin," Hicok writes: "I've never been able to understand the use of heroin, not in moral but practical terms. It is, for me, beyond the pale. I think of heroin addicts as graced with rare stupidity and courage, the inability to avoid, or willingness to embrace, certain dissolution and possible death. The intent of 'Heroin' is to present something of the physical seduction of the drug for someone who, in the time-frame of the poem, gives it up. The poem was also an opportunity to consider a bond that compels movement toward a different way of life, a stunning, and often unsuccessful, outcome of love.

"Lies, all lies. For in the simplest sense the poem was how I chose to follow, in a particular moment, a phrase that occurred to me but was later removed—'suppose you had a taste for it, this tampering/with blood.' Whatever exegesis I might apply, the poem is simply a vehicle for my curiosity, an attempt to use the animating qualities of poetry to give flesh to that supposition."

PAUL HOOVER was born in Harrisonburg, Virginia, in 1946. He is the author of six books of poetry, including *Viridian* (University of Georgia Press, 1997) and *The Novel: A Poem* (New Directions, 1990). He has served as poet-in-residence at Columbia College, Chicago, since 1974. He is the editor of *Postmodern American Poetry* (Norton, 1994), an anthology, and co-editor with Maxine Chernoff of the literary magazine *New American Writing*. He is also the author of a novel, *Saigon, Illinois* (Vintage, 1988), a semi-autobiographical account of working as a conscientious objector in a Chicago hospital during the Vietnam war.

Of "California," Hoover writes: "My family had moved to the Bay Area five months ahead of me, so I drove alone from Chicago to San Francisco in late January. Many of the poem's physical details came to me during the final day, as I passed through Reno and descended the Sierras through a driving rainstorm into California. The change of topography and culture startled me: the green lushness of the farmlands near Sacramento and Davis, the steady rush of expensive cars—especially in contrast to the landscape's barrenness east of Reno. It seemed that I had entered another country, with its own vegetation and way of being. So the poem is essentially the record of a dazzled but ironic immigrant. One of our first trips as tourists of our new climate was up Mt. Tamalpais, where my son Julian found a gecko—new to us Chicagoans—sunning on a rock. In our town of Mill Valley, everyone was a screenwriter or clinical psychologist.

"The poem has no formal features to speak of. It is all seeing, which is what I was after following a period of employing formal games and dispersive composition."

CHRISTINE HUME was born in 1968 in Alaska. She received an MFA from Columbia University in 1993 and is now pursuing a Ph.D. in creative writing at the University of Denver. She has taught humanities, literature, and writing at Stuyvesant High School in New York City, Aims Community College in Colorado, and Colorado State University. She was the 1995 winner of the Writers at Work fellowship, which was judged by Heather McHugh. Her work has appeared in *Antioch Review, Indiana Review,* and *Ploughshares.*

Hume writes: "What I wanted to get at in 'Helicopter Wrecked on a Hill' was a kinaesthetic logic of accumulations born out of acceleration in language, but the poem just tosses off its analogues without regard for my intent. Ultimately my hope is that the poem communicates directly on its own terms."

HARRY HUMES was born in Girardville, Pennsylvania, in 1935. A graduate of Bloomsburg State College and the graduate writing program at the University of North Carolina at Greensboro, he currently teaches in the English department of Kutztown University, Pennsylvania. His most recent books of poetry were published by the University of Arkansas Press: *The Bottomland* (1995), *The Way Winter Works* (1995), and *Ridge Music* (1987). The University of Missouri Press published his *Winter Weeds* in 1983 and awarded it the Devins Award for Poetry that year. His poem "Calling in the Hawk" received the Theodore Roethke Prize from *Poetry Northwest* in 1984. He is founder (1983) and editor of the poetry magazine *Yarrow* and a recipient of several poetry grants from the Pennsylvania Council on the Arts, the most recent in 1996. He was also a National Endowment for the Arts Poetry Fellow in 1990.

Of "The Butterfly Effect," Humes writes: "Several years ago, I was reading James Gleick's book *Chaos* (1987) and came across the phrase 'the butterfly effect.' This is the notion that a butterfly flapping its wings in one place will cause violent weather thousands of miles away. I was fascinated and tucked it away in my mind. The words kept returning, but nothing came of it until one summer day in 1995 when they took hold of me with unusual resonance and force. I sat down and the poem eventually happened.

"At the heart of the poem is the contrast between the butterfly's gentle wings and the fantastic energy they generate over a distant landscape: 'a white blossom,' 'a man sleeps,' 'a pond of red carp' soon enough became a 'ripple,' 'a wind [that] knocks trees over,' 'children [who] no longer turn somersaults,' the deer that 'staggers, / starving, across the frozen river.' Contrast is further suggested through the butterfly's small wings that become the 'bright wing of the sky.'

"I might add, too, that other poets echo throughout the poem: Ezra

Pound, whose translation of Rihaku's 'The River Merchant's Wife: A Letter' I carried with me for years, loving its rhythms and serenity. In 'bo tree,' 'horizon,' and 'pianos' are present Theodore Roethke, Ted Hughes, and W. H. Auden.

"I am always surprised and gratified when words, echoes, snatches of sounds that I've carried around in my head for years suddenly and inexplicably fall into place, and, if I am lucky, fall into an inviting place."

DON HYMANS was born in New Jersey in 1970. He is a graduate of Lafayette College (1992) and the University of Iowa Writers' Workshop (1994). He has received a New Jersey State Council on the Arts fellowship in literature. He has completed a manuscript of poems entitled *The Desert Ambulance.* He lives and works as an editor in New York City.

Of "Passacaglia," Hymans writes: "A passacaglia is a variation form of music (originally a dance) in which the theme, stretching over several bars, is continually repeated, usually but not necessarily always in the mischievous bass. Some examples include Bach's for organ, Couperin's for harpsichord, Hindemith's for viola, and Britten's from *Peter Grimes.*"

LAWSON FUSAO INADA was born in Fresno, California, in 1938. He was incarcerated in American internment camps in California, Arkansas, and Colorado during World War II. His most recent books of poetry are *Legends from Camp* (Coffee House Press, 1993), which received the American Book Award, and *Drawing the Line* (Coffee House Press, 1997). He is a professor of English at Southern Oregon State College.

Of "Making It Stick," Inada writes: "Basho, of course, is the author of the final 'bumper sticker'; he'd probably smile about contributing to this medium. As for the other 'stickers,' well, Basho himself might say: 'It depends on what kind of car, where it is, and who's driving.' "

RICHARD JACKSON is a professor of English at the University of Tennessee in Chattanooga where he has won several teaching awards and directs the undergraduate Meacham Creative Writing Workshops. He is the author of three books of poems, most recently *Alive All Day* (Cleveland State, 1992), two books of criticism from the University of Alabama Press, and *Double Vision,* an anthology of Slovene poetry (Aleph, 1994). He is on the staff of the Vermont College MFA program and also edits *Poetry Miscellany* and *malarevija.* He has been a Fulbright exchange poet in the former Yugoslavia. He is a member of the Slovene PEN Sarajevo Committee and has lectured widely in Eastern Europe.

Of "The Poem That Was Once Called 'Desperate' But Is Now Striving to Become the Perfect Love Poem," Jackson writes: "True to its title, the poem went through several stages, and also true to its title, it of course ultimately failed in its practical aim. For me, poetry is, as Longinus wrote centuries ago, a means of transport, the root meaning of metaphor—it takes me someplace other than where and what I am. This poem is ultimately, I guess, about the possibility of poetry—or the possibility of language. At the end of *Speak, Memory,* Nabokov describes how, waiting to depart for America, he could see, among the roofs of the city, behind a clothesline, the huge smokestack of the ship that would take him, 'as something in a scrambled picture—Find What the Sailor Has Hidden—that the finder cannot unsee once it has been seen.' Poetry gives us this new vision we cannot unsee; it is the boat, ready to transport us anywhere, to make new discoveries, and the boat includes the whole picture it is linked to, not just the isolated object, and that picture might include references to Catullus, Aeschylus, Sappho, street scenes, a dinner, etc.

"Byron uses the word 'mobility' to describe the self-corrective manner of writing (which lies behind this poem) in *Don Juan,* and the word in Italian has a number of rich associations. After all, as the aria goes in Verdi's *Rigoletto—La Donna e mobile*—the woman is fickle, as fickle, he goes on, as thistledown in the wind. But all of opera is in a sense mobile: one aria cuts across another in a series of competing emotions and allegiances, and melodies begin to diverge and come together. I hope this poem has that sort of multiple perspective: language and the heart, language and the mind, language and language—like competing voices."

GRAY JACOBIK was born in Newport News, Virginia, in 1944. She is an associate professor of English at Eastern Connecticut State University in Willimantic, Connecticut. She received her education at Goddard College and Brandeis University. At Brandeis she studied with Allen Grossman, Frank Bidart, and Sharon Olds. The recipient of fellowships from the National Endowment for the Arts (1993) and the Connecticut Commission on the Arts (1996), she won the first Emily Dickinson Poetry Prize offered by Universities West Press (1996).

Jacobik writes: " 'Dust Storm' began with the image of contrails, that ephemeral twentieth-century aerial scarring. I remember being haunted by the sight of two contrails crossing. I have never been to Wyoming, so much of this poem is romantic and erotic fantasy, although I have lived on the prairie and that landscape lives in me.

Writing this, I paid more attention to sound than to sense, thinking only to capture a particular state of mind or a condition of being connected with thwarted desire and a longing that is displaced onto the landscape. It seems to me that when the erotic is suppressed we feel our bodies spiral and glide, and so become 'out of element.' "

GEORGE KALAMARAS was born in Chicago in 1956. After living in Colorado and upstate New York, he returned to the Midwest and is currently an associate professor of English and director of creative writing at Indiana University—Purdue University at Fort Wayne. During 1994, he spent several months in India on a Fulbright Indo–U.S. Advanced Research Fellowship. His book on Hindu mysticism and Western rhetoric, *Reclaiming the Tacit Dimension: Symbolic Form in the Rhetoric of Silence,* was published by State University of New York Press in 1994. He has published two chapbooks of poetry, *Heart Without End* (Leaping Mountain Press, 1986) and *Beneath the Breath* (Tilton House, 1988). In 1993, he received a poetry fellowship from the National Endowment for the Arts. He lives in Fort Wayne, Indiana, with his wife, the writer Mary Ann Cain.

Kalamaras writes: "I wrote 'Mud' after spending several months in India during 1994. I've practiced yogic meditation for many years and have written extensively on the relationship between Hindu mysticism and Western language and poetic theory. During my stay in India, I focused my research primarily on *sadhus* (Hindu holy men), interviewing them and observing their practices firsthand at their ashrams, as well as researching the philosophy of their practices in Indian libraries.

"India has a long, rich tradition of high spiritual practice. At the same time, like any country, it has its share of social problems. In this poem I explore some of the social inequities I encountered during my travels. It's often easy for people (especially travelers) to point a wary finger at social inequities that arise in another country, especially when that country is significantly different from their own. However, in this poem I tried to explore some of these inequities (with a special emphasis on the plight of women in India) while also examining one's own implication in these or similar injustices.

"One term in the poem that may be unfamiliar is 'gherao,' which refers to a coercive tactic in India where workers surround and detain an employer on his own premises until their demands are met. However, in using this term I add a bit of a surreal twist, which I hope helps express the strangeness one often experiences during foreign travel.

'Mud' is part of a completed manuscript of poems, *The Theory and Function of Mangoes,* devoted to my experiences in India."

JENNIFER L. KNOX was born in Lancaster, California (that's where the space shuttle lands), in 1968. She received her undergraduate degree from the University of Iowa and has worked as a hotel maid, telemarketer, road crew flag girl, medical records clerk, teacher, and most recently advertising copywriter in Milwaukee, Wisconsin, where she lives with the writer Sean McNally.

Of "The Bright Light of Responsibility," Knox writes: "I enjoyed writing this poem, and it's all true. While teaching at a bank teller training school, I was constantly amazed that people who managed to drive cars, use microwave ovens, etc., could have the most bizarre conceptions of right and wrong. The cruelest ones never seemed to get in trouble. The speaker suggests a more private, comparatively dignified kind of self-abuse. Keep your hands as clean as possible and don't accidentally kill anyone on the way home."

PHILIP KOBYLARZ was born in Peoria, Illinois, in 1967, and has lived mostly in the West and Midwest. He attended Arizona State University and the University of Iowa Writers' Workshop. His poems have appeared in *Epoch, The Paris Review,* and *The Denver Quarterly.* He now teaches language and American culture in Marseilles, France.

Kobylarz writes: "What began as a thumbnail sketch of both a memory and a mood, then became a failed attempt at blank verse, turned into an extended meditation on the city as persona, loosely incorporating and confusing personal experience with the biographical details of Edwin Arlington Robinson. After several drafts and with the keen advice of the editor of the magazine in which it first appeared, the poem attempts to be, if not a last will, then a kind of testament of the Richard Cory who inhabits us all."

YUSEF KOMUNYAKAA was born in Bogalusa, Louisiana, in 1947. He served with the United States Army in Vietnam and was a correspondent and editor of *The Southern Cross.* He has taught at Indiana University and at Washington University in St. Louis. His books include *Copacetic* (1984), *I Apologize for the Eyes in My Head* (1986), *Dien Cai Dau* (1988), *Magic City* (1992), and *Neon Vernacular* (Wesleyan, 1993). *Neon Vernacular* was awarded the Kingsley Tufts Award in addition to the 1994 Pulitzer Prize.

Of "Jeanne Duval's Confession," Komunyakaa writes: "Having read Baudelaire's poems through the years, when I started thinking of his tormented muse, Jeanne Duval, she defined herself as natural subject matter. How could I not write about her, about the tension in these two lives? Their love-hate relationship became the foundation for much of Baudelaire's work, especially *Les Fleurs du mal*. His creativity makes us embrace Jeanne Duval as someone both virtuous and profane in the same breath. One can feel Baudelaire arm wrestling himself—there is a system of push and pull, moments of elation are etched out, almost like a tide, roaring in and rushing out. He worked with a canvas composed of foresight, enlightenment, and contradiction. Jeanne Duval wanders through his poems like a ghost that refuses to be subdued; one has a feeling that often she made Baudelaire drunk with words. I wanted to give emotional flesh to that ghost. I could not have written this poem in any other way because there she was speaking, through my mouth."

ELIZABETH KOSTOVA was born in 1964 and was educated in Tennessee and North Carolina and at Yale University; she has studied writing with Eddie Francisco, Peter Matthiessen, and John Barth. She has received the Wallace Fiction Prize at Yale University, a Charles Cinnamon Grant, a North Carolina Poetry Society Award, and an award from the North Carolina Fiction Syndicate. Her first book-length work, *1927: The Good-Natured Chronicle of a Journey,* an oral history/travel memoir with architect Anthony Lord, was published by the Captain's Bookshelf Press in October 1995. She lives in Philadelphia, where she teaches in Drexel University's intensive English language program. She is currently at work on a book-length manuscript of poems, a book of interviews, and a novel, *The Historian.*

Kostova writes: "I've become interested in the outcome of quick, meditative strokes of writing—the Zen calligrapher's rapid journey over paper. What does this writing 'hand' do, left to its own devices? I write both fiction and poetry and am frequently engaged in long deliberative sessions of composition—constructing cities, conversations, and lives, working along stretches of plot toward a visible horizon. In other, antidotal, sessions, experimental writing practice—a kind of rush at the page—has become for me a way to break up the sediment, jump the track, remember play. One of the intriguing results of this leap onto paper is a blurring of the distinctions among genres. The writing hand disregards choices between fictions and observations, poetry and prose; its medium is simply words. It doesn't compose; it writes.

"In 1994 I started an evening writing group with friends and faculty members at a local college. For several months, we met occasionally to write together in a basement classroom and to read aloud immediately afterward from what we'd written. During these evenings, we took turns proposing writing exercises. In that setting, I found my spontaneous writing practice acquiring a most un-Zen-like but interesting edge of performance anxiety. Add a little adrenaline to a little meditation and what do you get? Writing?

" 'Suddenly I Realized I Was Sitting' is my version of an exercise I proposed one night: Write for five minutes using the sentence 'Suddenly I realized I was sitting on a volcano.' I hadn't planned any response to this sentence, but as I wrote I felt a stinging awareness of the act of writing, an out-of-body view of the ability of words to simulate reality. I had the sensation you sometimes get in the midst of ebbing, flowing conversation, a revelation of the way words are suddenly charged with a life of their own. The people in my poem don't exist except there; they aren't based on anybody; I don't have any tidy little anecdotes to relate about them—'Phil is a man I worked with for two years in a fondue restaurant who told me one day how much he hated his sister for dying'—nothing like that, just words. Suddenly, as I wrote, I realized we were all sitting on a volcano: language."

DENISE LEVERTOV was born in London, England, in 1923. She served as a nurse in World War II. She came to the United States in 1948 and was naturalized in 1955. Having retired from Stanford after teaching there since 1981, she now lives year-round in Seattle. Her books include *Collected Earlier Poems, 1940–1960* (1979), *Breathing the Water* (1987), and *A Door in the Hive* (1989), all from New Directions. Her new collection is *Sands of the Well* (1996).

Of "The Change," Levertov writes: "There are poems that give a foothold for authorial comment, I know—but this isn't one of them. Anything I could say would only be paraphrase, which I hope this poem doesn't need."

LARRY LEVIS was born in Fresno, California, in 1946. He grew up as a ranch boy in the small town of Selma, the "raisin capital of the universe." He started writing poetry at Fresno State College, where he studied with Philip Levine, who became a lifelong friend. "That an unathletic, acne-ridden virgin who owned the slowest car in town should at age sixteen decide to become a poet struck [Levis] as both outrageous and perfectly right," Levine writes. Levis went on to receive his MA from Syracuse University and his Ph.D. from the University of Iowa. His books include *Wrenching Crew* (1972), *The Afterlife* (1977), *The Dollmaker's Ghost* (1981), *Winter Stars* (1985), and *The Widening Spell of the Leaves* (University of Pittsburgh Press, 1991). A new book, *Elegy,* will be published by the University of Pittsburgh Press. In addition to serving as director of the creative writing program at the University of Utah, he taught poetry at California State College in Los Angeles and at the University of Iowa. At the time of his death he was a professor of English at Virginia Commonwealth University in Richmond. Philip Levine writes: "For thirty years, his devotion to the art had served as my inspiration and model. . . . When I am weary of the mediocrity or smallness of so much that passes for poetry, I go to Larry's work and revive my belief in the value of the art we shared. . . . It was easy to take from Larry, for his whole vision of why we are here on this earth had to do with giving." Larry Levis died in May 1996.

MATTHEW LIPPMAN was born in New York City in 1965. He graduated from Hobart and William Smith Colleges in 1987. In 1990 he received his MFA from the Writers' Workshop at the University of Iowa. Two years later he was awarded that university's James Michener/Paul Engle Poetry Fellowship. He has taught creative writing at the DIA Center for the Arts, Columbia University's summer program for high school students, and Westchester Community College. Currently he is at Teachers College, working toward a master's in Education, High School English. His poems have appeared in the *Seneca Review, Iowa Review, Indiana Review,* and *The American Poetry Review.* His manuscript *Hallelujah Terrible* awaits publication.

Lippman writes: " 'Hallelujah Terrible' started with the first line and then just took off. It was one of those poems that just happens. I have no idea where it came from and no idea what it means. I do know that when I got into it, when I was writing, I was aware of keeping close to the theme of 'no other man.' That was the refrain that held things together. Deborah Tall, editor of the *Seneca Review,* said she liked the classical nature of the poem. I like it that she said that because I don't think it was my intention to make it a 'classical poem.' I'm not very concerned with form or even motivated by it. Yet I know what Deborah was talking about. There is some crazy kind of architecture in the poem that, even now, is identifiable and exciting. I like it that the spirit feels somewhat kooky but at the same time focused. I also like it that the writing of 'Hallelujah Terrible,' as with most of my poems, took a very short time—fifteen minutes perhaps—and so everything was quick and free.

"This has been my desire all along with my work—to be able to write out of my head, totally inspired, and at the same time to stay as grounded and accessible as possible. A lot of times there is a bird chirping too loud or something on the TV or some wall in my head that distracts me. Not with 'Hallelujah Terrible.' It was there all the way to get-go."

BETH LISICK was born in San Jose, California, in 1968. After graduating from the University of California at Santa Cruz in 1991, she began reading her poems and stories in bars, nightclubs, and coffee shops around the country. Her poems have been published in *Clockwatch Review* and *Revival: Spoken Word from Lollapalooza* (Manic D. Press, 1995). Her recordings have been featured on the compilations *Meow: Spoken Word from the Black Cat* and *Market Street: Live from Cafe du Nord*. A member of the San Francisco slam team, she participated in the 1995 and 1996 National Poetry Slams and was featured at the 1994 Lollapalooza Festival and the 1995 South by Southwest Music Festival. She is the author of *Monkey Girl* (Manic D. Press, 1997). She lives in Oakland, California. "Empress of Sighs" was her first published poem.

Of "Empress of Sighs," Lisick writes: "It was written for parents who retire to gated communities of steel-framed homes and former television stars who drink nightcaps in their pajamas while gardenias bloom in the desert."

KHALED MATTAWA was born in Benghazi, Libya, in 1964, and emigrated to the United States in 1979. He went to high school in Louisiana, and earned bachelor's degrees in political science and economics from the University of Tennessee at Chattanooga. He has an MA in English and an MFA in creative writing from Indiana University. An assistant professor of English and Creative Writing at California State University, Northridge, he was the Alfred Hodder Fellow at Princeton University in 1995–96. He is the author of *Ismailia Eclipse* (Sheep Meadow Press, 1995). He is also the translator of two books of contemporary Arabic poetry, Hatif Janabi's *Questions and Their Retinue* (University of Arkansas Press) and Fadhil Al-Azzawi's *In Every Well a Joseph Is Weeping* (Quarterly Review of Literature). He received a Guggenheim Fellowship in poetry in 1997.

Of "Heartsong," Mattawa writes: "I wrote this poem on a rainy spring night. I had been reading Rumi and St. John of the Cross for months then, along with a number of Arab poets I was translating. The poets I was reading drew me with their earnestness and passion. They made irony and reminiscence look like mere checkpoints along the road to truth. And so on that spring night I wanted, or felt ready, to say something unabashedly without resignation or surrender, and what came out was the sense of yearning the poem expressed. I do not recall getting on top of the house as the poem states, but I remember having that vision: I really saw myself in the rain standing on the roof chanting the poem's anaphora. Writing the poem did not take a long time, and very few revisions were required. But it stayed with me for weeks as I found myself chanting 'Come love, come love,' as I walked down the street or the aisles of a supermarket."

WILLIAM MATTHEWS was born in Cincinnati, Ohio, in 1942. His recent book of poems, *Time and Money* (Houghton Mifflin, 1995), received the National Book Critics Circle Award in poetry. A book of translations, *The Mortal City: 100 Epigrams of Martial,* appeared from Ohio Review Books in 1995. He has finished work on a translation of Horace's satires. He is a professor of English at the City College of the City University of New York.

Of "Vermin," Matthews writes: "We humans like to be at the top of the food chain, the pyramids, the ski lift, the A list, the heap. But suppose we're just another rung on the ladder, and a foot as heavy as a human foot gets planted on us."

JOSIP NOVAKOVICH was born in Daruvar, Croatia, in 1956. He is assistant professor of English at the University of Cincinnati. His books include new collections of stories, *Yold,* and essays, *Apricots from Chernobyl,* both from Graywolf (1995). His poems have appeared in *Southern Review, Poet Lore,* and *Quarterly West,* his prose in *Antaeus, The Paris Review,* and *The New York Times Magazine.*

Novakovich writes: "Occasionally I write prose poems as fiction études. I wrote 'Shadow' as a meditation on how metaphors are made. My two-year-old son called shadows puddles and puddles shadows, and his cognitive dilemma as to how to label the phenomena struck me as charming—it transposed me onto a way of learning how to put words and images together anew and charmed up what at the moment worked as an epiphany. Why not call a shadow a puddle of darkness? Generally, I don't like family poems, but here I couldn't resist the clear family lesson in how metaphors could be made. The cognitive processes of infants and toddlers strike me as akin to what I imagine poets should do—see things as though for the first time. First I was about to play with the shadow the metaphors in a historical poem about the Byzantines gouging the eyes of a defeated Macedonian army, but the metaphors assumed an independence and liveliness of their own, so I cut them out and made a vignette, where for the rhythms I didn't rely on a meter but on a succession of alternative images."

GEOFFREY NUTTER was born in California in 1968. He attended San Francisco State University and the University of Iowa. While there he was awarded the Academy of American Poets Prize. He lives in New York City, where he teaches English as a Second Language at Bronx Community College. He has taught creative writing at Columbia University's high school summer writing program, and has also taught poetry to children in public schools and to mentally ill adults through the Bronx Council on the Arts WritersCorps program. He wrote *A Summer Evening* while working as a security guard at the Metropolitan Museum of Art. His poems have appeared in the *Colorado Review, Iowa Journal of Cultural Studies,* and *Iowa Review,* and he has had a short story in *Five Fingers Review.*

Nutter writes: "These are four of forty-eight parts of a larger poem called *A Summer Evening.* All of the poems are titled with the times of their completion. The form of each piece is prescribed, but as with the titles I wanted there to be an element of randomness in their composition. I was trying to get at something more interesting than what my own will and desire could yield. I called the poem *A Summer Evening* because a summer evening is like a beautiful enclosure, identical in form to its counterparts, yet containing different things. This is dedicated to my brother, Ethan Nutter."

CATIE ROSEMURGY was born in Madison, Wisconsin, in 1969, and grew up in Escanaba, Michigan. She attended Macalester College and received her MFA from the University of Alabama. Her work has recently appeared in *Indiana Review* and *Cream City Review.*

Of "Mostly Mick Jagger," Rosemurgy writes: "I was reading a magazine article about the Rolling Stones' latest concert tour, and the article quoted the guitar player, Keith Richards, as saying that, for some people, there has always been the sun, the moon, and the Rolling Stones. The notion that I have never known a world without the

Rolling Stones struck me, and I began to wonder how one is affected by a lifetime of exposure to the image of a very unique-looking man in very unique, occasionally pink, outfits."

CLARE ROSSINI was born in St. Paul, Minnesota, in 1954. She was educated at the College of St. Benedict, the Iowa Writers' Workshop, and Columbia University, where she received a Ph.D. in literature in 1991. Her first book of poems, *Winter Morning with Crow*, was selected by Donald Justice for the 1996 Akron Poetry Prize and will appear in 1997 from the University of Akron Press. She teaches at Carleton College in Northfield, Minnesota, as well as in the Vermont College low-residency MFA program.

Rossini writes: " 'Valediction' was written a few months after I had given birth to a stillborn child. I had been trying to write coherently of that event, without much luck, when one hot July morning, I pounded out 'Valediction' in almost finished form. I wrote it so quickly, in fact, that I didn't trust the poem for several months. In retrospect, I suppose that the genesis of 'Valediction' provides another example of how, in the composing process, one thing often leads to another; in this case, how the loss of the child tapped into other, older angers and griefs."

MARY RUEFLE was born in McKeesport, Pennsylvania, in 1952. She has received a National Endowment for the Arts Fellowship and a Whiting Writer's Award. Her publications include four books of poems: *Memling's Veil* (1982), *Life Without Speaking* (1987), *The Adamant* (1989), and *Cold Pluto* (Carnegie Mellon, 1996). She lives in Bennington, Vermont, and teaches in the MFA writing program at Vermont College.

Of "Topophilia," Ruefle writes: "The poem evolved in the process of writing it, as all my poems do. After the fact, it could be described as a monologue written in the voice of a housewife with a touch of agoraphobia. But why does agoraphobia have to be described in negative terms, a fear of being in the open? Why not a positive take on it, *love of spot?* Hence the title. I don't actually remember writing the poem, but I do remember I had been reading a life of Attila the Hun and had recently moved from a kind of cabin-shack into a fancy full-fledged house. I was still reeling from the changes, I guess. Maybe I felt like Attila; it's an aggressive poem written by someone basically lethargic."

HILLEL SCHWARTZ was born in Chicago in 1948. He works as an independent scholar and cultural historian, and he is a Senior Fellow at the

Millennium Institute in Arlington, Virginia. His research has taken him from the history of dieting in America (*Never Satisfied,* 1986) to *Century's End: A Cultural History of the Fin de Siècle from the 990s through the 1990s* (Doubleday, 1990). His most recent book, *The Culture of the Copy: Striking Likenesses, Unreasonable Facsimiles* (Zone, 1996), is a study of the social and ethical consequences of our facility at (and obsession with) copying. His work has been translated into German, Italian, Japanese, and Portuguese. He is currently conducting research toward a cultural history of noise in the modern West since about 1740.

MAUREEN SEATON was born in Elizabeth, New Jersey. She is the author of three books of poetry: *Furious Cooking* (University of Iowa Press, 1996), winner of the Iowa Prize for Poetry; *The Sea Among the Cupboards* (New Rivers, 1992); and *Fear of Subways* (Eighth Mountain Press, 1991). She has received grants from the Illinois Arts Council and the National Endowment for the Arts. Her poems have appeared in *The Atlantic, The Paris Review,* and *The New Republic.* She lives in Chicago.

Seaton writes: "I was playing with a very long line during a certain period and 'Fiddleheads' came about. Subject-wise: Sometimes I feel attached to strange things. In this case, it was a shipment of fiddlehead ferns I'd seen thrown into a pot then served beside steak and potatoes, the way the ferns looked when they first arrived, people melting butter on them afterward. I feel especially tender toward planet Earth. And, finally, I'm intrigued with perspective, how anything can change over time and space."

VIJAY SESHADRI was born in India in 1954 and came to America at the age of five. He grew up in Columbus, Ohio, attended Oberlin College, and has lived in many parts of the country, including the Oregon coast, where he spent five years working in the fishing and logging industries, and New York's Upper West Side, where he was a graduate student in Columbia's doctoral program in Middle Eastern Studies. A collection of his poems, *Wild Kingdom,* was published in 1996 by Graywolf. He now lives in Brooklyn with his wife and son, and earns his living as a magazine editor and freelance writer.

Of "Lifeline," Seshadri says: "The idea of writing a poem about someone lost in the woods had been in my mind for a while—I had once been lost in the Oregon woods for about five hours; though, except for a bad ten minutes or so, I was always convinced I'd find my way out. But the poem didn't come to life until I conceived of it as a long block of language, somewhat like a Richard Serra sculpture. The problem of writing the poem then became the more manageable problem of articulating the surface of the block. I wanted to resist the inevitable allegorical pressures of the subject, while appropriating, if I could, the energy behind those pressures. The plot of the poem unspools along the lines of force created by this tension. Writing it was a pleasure. I felt while doing so that the only thing required of me was that I get the details right, that everything else would take care of itself, which is a rare feeling in my life as a writer, and one whose memory I savor to this day."

STEVEN SHERRILL was born in Mooresville, North Carolina, in 1961. His formal education began with a vocational diploma in welding and culminated, temporarily, with an MFA from the University of Iowa. Obsessive by nature, he is driven to produce stories and poems, and—with great pleasure—paintings of questionable quality. His work has appeared in *Farmer's Market, Georgia Review, Hayden's Ferry Review, Mudfish, Plum Review, Seattle Review,* and *Santa Barbara Review.* At the moment he is seeking a publisher for his manuscript, *The Sleep of Barabbas.* He lives near Chicago with his wife, the poet Barbara Campbell. Their daughter, Maude Eleanor Rose, was born in July 1996.

Of "Katyn Forest," Sherrill writes: "A radio story about Stalin's massacre of Polish officers and civilians and the mass graves planted over with apple trees in Kosygori made me cry. My first impulse was to respond with a painting. But as happens often, my imagination far outstrips my technical skills, and today the unfinished painting—a landscape of leaning apple trees, blue sky, and a split fruit sun, colors somewhere between ominous and cartoonish—hangs at the foot of my basement stairs.

"I am obsessive, and driven to research whatever occupies my mind. Fortunately I had access to a fine library, and there was a wealth of material on the incident at Katyn Forest. Ample text detailing the horrors. Photograph after numbing photograph of bones in disarray. But what pulled this event across decades, what brought it to poignant life inside me, were the personal articles gathered from the bodies: a stamp collection, pictures of children, letters full of hope and love and fear. Twenty-one thousand, eight hundred and fifty-six bodies."

CHARLES SIMIC was born in Belgrade, Yugoslavia, in 1939, and emigrated to the United States in 1953. Since 1967 he has published about sixty books in this country and abroad. His latest poetry collections include *Walking the Black Cat, A Wedding in Hell,* and *Hotel Insomnia,* all from Harcourt Brace. He won the Pulitzer Prize in 1990 for his book of prose poems *The World Doesn't End.* Three volumes of his prose have appeared in the University of Michigan Press's Poets on Poetry Series, most recently *The Unemployed Fortune-Teller* (1994). Awarded a MacArthur Fellowship in 1984, he was the guest editor of *The Best American Poetry 1992.* Since 1973 he has lived in New Hampshire.

Of "The Something," Simic writes: "This is one of those poems written around a single word. An ordinary, often-used word which suddenly became odd, unrecognizable, puzzling, haunting, and so forth. One is always looking for *something,* thinking of *something,* pointing at *something.* What the hell is this *something?* one asks oneself one day. A *something* that doesn't seem to have any other name.

"Well, there was plenty there for me to play with."

CHARLIE SMITH was born in Moultrie, Georgia, in 1947. He grew up in the South, traveled, and has lived for a number of years in New York City. He has published four books of poems: *Red Roads* (Dutton, 1987, National Poetry Series), *Indistinguishable from the Darkness* (Norton, 1990), *The Palms* (Norton, 1993), and *Before and After* (Norton, 1995). His new book, *Life on Earth* (from which "Beds" is taken), is forthcoming from Norton. He has also published five novels, including *The Lives of the Dead, Shine Hawk,* and the recent *Cheap Tickets to Heaven,* and a collection of novellas, *Crystal River.*

Of "Beds," Smith writes: "I was writing a lot of poems that came out of long-after-midnight walks I took throughout the city. The poems were cavalcades, kind of mutating strip-search kinds of things, rambling, dictated to myself over my shoulder as I ran through the streets, nervous, bouncy, capering, fast type of poems without much stop and staring in them and once, on a late night as I was walking with a friend, she said why not beds? So I gave it a try."

LEON STOKESBURY was born in Oklahoma City in 1945. He grew up in southeast Texas and graduated from Lamar State College of Technology in 1968. His first book of poems, *Often in Different Landscapes,* was a co-winner of the first Associated Writing Programs Poetry Competition in 1975 and was published by the University of Texas Press in 1976. His latest book of poems, *Autumn Rhythm: New and Selected Poems,* appeared in 1996 from the University of Arkansas Press. He has taught poetry and creative writing in universities in a half dozen southern states, and since 1987 has taught in the graduate writing program at Georgia State University in Atlanta.

Stokesbury writes: "Janis Joplin was in no way a celebrity when I knew her. Although I was not aware of it then, 1966 was the last year in Beaumont, Texas, that the world would seem unchanging. All the forces that were being brought to bear on American life in the cities and on the coasts, the forces of what we call 'the sixties,' were seemingly held off from southeast Texas for that last year. Or so it seems in my memory. There was little in Beaumont and Port Arthur to keep Janis Joplin there once her relationship had broken up. You could say she spent the previous five years trying to get away from the place. It does seem like another world today. Like a dream. It may be difficult for anyone reading 'Evening's End' in the nineties to realize how little the incidents described in the poem meant to me while they were happening. Indeed, I did not even think of them until two years later when *Cheap Thrills* and Big Brother and the Holding Company burst upon rock music. I can still remember the moment I first turned over the album cover and saw Janis Joplin's photograph on the back. I was truly amazed that the tiny, shy woman I had known at Lamar was this obvious genius on the record. She must have been walking around Beaumont in a state of complete and constant alienation. She must have been very lonely.

"The poem itself is written with as much simplicity as I could muster. It begins in the present and then tells its story in a narrative of three or four flashback scenes. What poetry there is comes, I think, from the line breaks and stanza breaks, the condensation of language, and from the story itself. The last line is from *Hamlet*."

MARK STRAND was born in Canada of American parents in 1934. After many years of teaching at the University of Utah, he now lives in Baltimore and teaches at Johns Hopkins. He has held a MacArthur Foundation Fellowship. His most recent books are *Dark Harbor* (1993) and *The Continuous Life* (1990), both from Knopf, and a monograph on Edward Hopper (Ecco). He has also published short stories and translations from the Spanish and the Portuguese. He was the guest editor of *The Best American Poetry 1991*.

Of "Morning, Noon and Night," Strand writes: "I don't recall much about the composition of this poem. I worked on it over a long stretch of time, pulling it out of a drawer, looking at it, putting it back in a drawer.

That sort of thing. The end, getting it right—if I ever did—took lots of rewriting. A delicate, unpleasant paradox imbedded in few words."

JACK TURNER was born in Chattanooga, Tennessee, in 1947. He worked in radio as an announcer, writer, and producer before earning his Ph.D. in English at the University of South Carolina, where he won the Academy of American Poets Award in 1989. In addition to poems, stories, and essays, he has published a book, *Murdoch vs. Freud* (Lang, 1993), about Iris Murdoch's quarrel with Freudian psychology. He is currently chief technical writer for the Delaware Office of Information Services and adjunct professor of English at Wesley College in Dover.

Turner writes: " 'The Plan' speaks for itself. However, I am well aware of the desperate plight of many migrant workers, and my reference to 'some half-starved Guatemalan' is in no way meant to be derogatory. It is simply a reflection of a disgraceful situation that cries out to be remedied."

KAREN VOLKMAN was born in Miami in 1967 and educated at New College, Syracuse University, and the University of Houston. Her first book of poems, *Crash's Law*, was selected by Heather McHugh for the National Poetry Series (Norton, 1996). She received a National Endowment for the Arts fellowship in poetry in 1993. Her poems have appeared in *Poetry, The Paris Review, The American Poetry Review, Partisan Review*, and *Chelsea;* "The Case" was selected by Adrienne Rich for *The Best American Poetry 1996.* She has received fellowships from the McDowell Colony, Yaddo, and the Bread Loaf Writers' Conference, and has reviewed books for *The Harvard Review, The Boston Review*, and *The Voice Literary Supplement.* Currently she lives in Brooklyn, teaches writing at New York University, and works with Teachers & Writers Collaborative, teaching poetry in the public schools.

Volkman writes: " 'Infernal' is a haywire memory poem about my peculiar birthplace, Miami. Written during a blizzard in my adopted Northeast, it attempts to capture the surreal character of south Florida's burlesque, blistered terrain. Formally, I borrowed one element from the ghazal—the disjunctive couplets—attracted by the notion of an ancient form employing what we tend to think of as a contemporary strategy: disjunction adding up to a sort of final dissociative sense. The 'revenant' is one of several demons who haunt my work; here, he is some kind of devil of obsessive memory. This landscape is of course an inner one as well—Miami in the world and in the mind—and it reflects what seems to me an inevitable extremity of terms as the consciousness takes in the shocks and traumas of a violent time."

DEREK WALCOTT was born in Saint Lucia, the West Indies, in 1930. His books of poems include *Another Life* (1973), *The Star-Apple Kingdom* (1979), *The Fortunate Traveller* (1982), *Midsummer* (1984), and *The Arkansas Testament* (1987), all from Farrar, Straus & Giroux. Walcott won a MacArthur Fellowship in 1981 and the Nobel Prize for literature in 1992. His recent works include *Omeros* (1990) and *The Bounty* (1997). He is the founder of the Trinidad Theater Workshop, and his plays have been produced by the New York Shakespeare Festival, the Mark Taper Forum in Los Angeles, and the Negro Ensemble Company. He has published four books of plays with Farrar, Straus & Giroux. He divides his time between Boston, where he teaches at Boston University, and Trinidad.

ROSANNA WARREN was born in Connecticut in 1953. She is an associate professor at Boston University, teaching in the University Professors Program and the Department of English. Her recent publications include a verse translation (with Stephen Scully) of Euripedes' *Suppliant Women* (Oxford, 1995), and a collection of poems, *Stained Glass* (Norton, 1993). She has taught poetry to prisoners at the Massachusetts Correctional Institute in Framingham. She has received awards from the Lila Wallace–Reader's Digest Fund and the Guggenheim Foundation.

Of "Diversion," Warren writes: "The poem plays with time and memory of forms: the large memory in which ancient myth still presides and certain cadences hold consecrated place; and the shards of personal memory, our human transience and fragmentation."

LEWIS WARSH was born in New York City in 1944. His most recent books are a volume of stories, *Money Under the Table* (Trip Street Press, 1997); a book of poems, *Avenue of Escape* (Long News, 1995); a book-length poem, *Private Agenda,* with drawings by Pamela Lawton (Hornswoggle Press, 1996); and a memoir, with photographs, *Bustin's Island '68* (Granary Books, 1996). He is also the author of two novels, *A Free Man* (Sun & Moon, 1991) and *Agnes & Sally* (Fiction Collective, 1984). He was the editor of *The World,* the literary magazine of the Poetry Project, from 1992 to 1994, and is currently editor and publisher of United Artists Books. He has taught at the Poetry Project and the Naropa Institute, and is an adjunct professor in writing at Long Island University in Brooklyn. He has received grants from the National Endowment for the Arts, the New York Foundation for the Arts, and the Fund for Poetry, and in 1994 won the Jerome J. Shestack Prize from *The American Poetry Review*.

Warsh writes: " 'Downward Mobility' poses a question in different forms: how to act, what are the consequences of what you do, is it better not to act at all. All routes tend to point in the same direction, so why not do something extreme, if you're going to do anything. There seem to be a lot of passive-aggressive feelings in the poem, and not just beneath the surface, but at the heart of the poem is the fear of losing someone if I act one way and not another, as well as fear of unknown places, being alone, growing old. There's a kind of anti-utopian sentiment in the last lines—think of yourself, not someone else—but maybe that's just a last resort, what you do when you have no other choice. The poem was written out of the feeling of being in a corner, and of not feeling much connection with what was happening—that it was happening to 'me.' I'd like to think that possibly the poem itself is the answer to the question of how to act and maybe writing poetry or creating anything is the only viable response to a negative situation: war, homelessness, exile, an oppressive relationship—whatever."

TERENCE WINCH, the son of Irish immigrants, was born in New York City in 1945. He moved to Washington, D.C., in 1971. He performs and records with a traditional Irish band called Celtic Thunder, for which he writes songs and tunes; he has recorded three albums with Celtic Thunder. Among his books are *Contenders* (Story Line Press, 1989), a collection of short stories, and several books of poetry, including *Irish Musicians/American Friends* (Coffee House Press, 1986), which won an American Book Award, and *The Great Indoors* (Story Line Press, 1995), which won the Columbia Book Award. In 1992 he won a poetry fellowship from the National Endowment for the Arts. He works for the National Museum of the American Indian, the newest Smithsonian museum, in Washington, D.C.

Of "Shadow Grammar," Winch writes: "I wish I could remember now with authority where some of the elements in this poem came from, but I can't. The sources of certain aspects of the poem, though, I can guess at. My mother was born and raised on a farm in Ireland, and I'm sure that 'farm houses of my past' points back to those origins. In the last few years, parenthood has made me a reader of children's books, which I wasn't as a child, and the fairy-tale language of the second stanza seems influenced by that recent reading. The title suggests the parallel universe created by any work of art."

EVE WOOD was born in Los Angeles in 1967. She received BFA and MFA degrees in visual art from the California Institute of the Arts. In 1992 she attended Sarah Lawrence College as a Jacob Javits Scholar. In 1995 she was a scholar at the Bread Loaf Writers' Conference. Her poems have appeared in *Exquisite Corpse, Poetry, Antioch Review, Alaska Quarterly Review, The New Republic,* and *Nimrod.* She is currently working for the Getty Research Institute in their photo studies program. She is at work on a book of stories entitled *God Is a Bullet.*

Of "Recognition," Wood writes: "This poem began as a formal apology to a friend of mine who was sick with breast cancer. She recovered from the cancer, but the friendship had dissolved. When I finished the poem, I realized I had written my way out of grief, and was in fact attempting to formulate an apology to myself, a means by which *I* might move beyond the experience of losing someone dear to me. The poem was my container for loss."

CHARLES WRIGHT was born in Pickwick Dam, Tennessee, in 1935. Educated at Davidson College, he served in the army for four years, then attended the Writers' Workshop at the University of Iowa. He lectured at the universities of Rome and Padua under the Fulbright program. He has received fellowships from the National Endowment for the Arts and the Guggenheim Foundation and won a PEN award for his translation of Eugenio Montale's *The Storm and Other Things.* He is a professor of English at the University of Virginia at Charlottesville, where he lives with his family. In 1996 he was awarded the Lenore Marshall poetry prize for his book *Chickamauga* (Farrar, Straus & Giroux, 1995). "Disjecta Membra" is the concluding poem in his latest collection, *Black Zodiac* (Farrar, Straus & Giroux, 1997).

Of "Disjecta Membra," Wright notes: "All that's necessary—and all that I really want to say—is that the title of this poem comes from Guido Ceronetti's *The Science of the Body:* 'These fragments are the *disjecta membra* [scattered parts] of an elusive, coveted and vaguely scented knowledge.' "

DEAN YOUNG was born in Columbia, Pennsylvania, in 1955. He is an associate professor at Loyola University in Chicago. He has published three books of poems: *Design with X* (1988) and *Beloved Infidel* (1992), both from Wesleyan, and *Strike Anywhere,* which Charles Simic selected for the Colorado Poetry Prize in 1995. His work has appeared in two previous editions of *The Best American Poetry.*

Of "Frottage," Young writes: "This poem grew out of an assignment I gave some students to begin a poem 'How terrible and goofy is life' (which none of them did) and the Max Ernst show in Chicago a few years ago. One of the aspects of surrealism I admire, and try to practice, is the readiness to welcome and use emergent forms and accidental discoveries. Frottage, as practiced by Ernst and many others, involved accentuation and juxtaposition of material churned up by near accident, by nearly unintentional and unintending processes. Somehow a lion comes charging out of an ink blot. What face do you see in the clouds? It seems to me that much of Ernst's art captures a disturbing silliness and terror, a fear that makes us giggle, a joke that is very scary. Finally I don't think the goofy and terrible are all that different."

MAGAZINES WHERE THE POEMS
WERE FIRST PUBLISHED

American Letters and Commentary, ed. Anna Rabinowitz. 850 Park Avenue, #5B, New York, New York 10021.

The American Poetry Review, eds. Stephen Berg, David Bonnano, and Arthur Vogelsang. 1721 Walnut Street, Philadelphia, Pennsylvania 19103.

Another Chicago Magazine, eds. Lee Webster and Barry Silesky. 3709 N. Kenmore, Chicago, Illinois 60613.

Arshile, ed. Mark Salerno. P.O. Box 3749, Los Angeles, California 90078.

Black Warrior Review, ed. Mark Drew. P.O. Box 2936, Tuscaloosa, Alabama, 35486-2936.

Chelsea, ed. Richard Foerster. P.O. Box 773 Cooper Station, New York, New York 10276.

Clockwatch Review, ed. James Plath. Department of English, Illinois Wesleyan University, Bloomington, Illinois 61702.

Colorado Review, poetry ed. Jorie Graham. Department of English, Colorado State University, 359 Eddy Building, Fort Collins, Colorado 80523.

Cream City Review, eds. Kristin Terwelp and Cynthia Belmont. Department of English, University of Wisconsin, Milwaukee, Wisconsin 53201.

Denver Quarterly, ed. Bin Ramke. Department of English, University of Denver, Denver, Colorado 80208.

Exquisite Corpse, ed. Andrei Codrescu. P.O. Box 25051, Baton Rouge, Louisiana 70894.

Gettysburg Review, ed. Peter Stitt. Gettysburg College, Gettysburg, Pennsylvania 17325.

Grand Street, ed. Jean Stein. 131 Varick Street, Room 906, New York, New York 10013.

Green Mountains Review, ed. Neil Shepard. Johnson State College, Johnson, Vermont 05656.

Hanging Loose, ed. Bob Hershon. 231 Wyckoff Street, Brooklyn, New York 11217.

Hudson Review, eds. Paula Deitz and Frederick Morgan. 684 Park Avenue, New York, New York 10021.

Indiana Review, ed. Shirley Stephenson. Indiana University, 316 N. Jordan Avenue, Bloomington, Indiana 47405.

Iowa Review, ed. David Hamilton. 308 EPB, University of Iowa, Iowa City, Iowa 52242-1408.

The Kenyon Review, ed. David Lynn. Kenyon College, Gambier, Ohio 43022.

Many Mountains Moving, eds. Marilyn Krysl and Naomi Horey. 420 22nd Street, Boulder, Colorado 80302.

Massachusetts Review, eds. Paul Jenkins and Anne Halley. Memorial Hall, University of Massachusetts, Amherst, Massachusetts 01003.

New Letters, eds. Bob Stewart and James McKinley. University of Missouri at Kansas City, Kansas City, Missouri 64110.

The New Republic, poetry ed. Mark Strand. 1220 19th Street NW, Washington, D.C. 20036.

The New York Review of Books, eds. Barbara Epstein and Robert Silvers. 250 West 57th Street, New York, New York 10107.

The New Yorker, poetry ed. Alice Quinn. 20 West 43rd Street, New York, New York 10036.

North American Review, ed. Peter Cooley. University of Northern Iowa, Cedar Falls, Iowa 50614.

The Paris Review, ed. Richard Howard. 541 East 72nd Street, New York, New York 10021.

Ploughshares, eds. Don Lee and David Daniel. Emerson College, 100 Beacon Street, Boston, Massachusetts 02116.

Poetry, ed. Joseph Parisi. 60 West Walton Street, Chicago, Illinois 60610.

Quarterly West, eds. Sally Thomas and Margot Schilpp. University of Utah, 317 Olpin Union, Salt Lake City, Utah 84112.

Santa Monica Review, ed. Lee Montgomery. Santa Monica College, 1900 Pico Boulevard, Santa Monica, California 90405.

Seneca Review, ed. Deborah Tall. Hobart and William Smith Colleges, Geneva, New York 14456-3397.

Shenandoah, eds. R. T. Williams and Lynn L. Leech. Troubadour Theater, 2nd Floor, Washington and Lee University, Lexington, Virginia 24450-0303.

The Times Literary Supplement, ed. Ferdinand Mount. Admiral House, 66–68 East Smithfield, London E1 9XY, England.

TriQuarterly, eds. Reginald Gibbons and Susan Hahn. 2020 Ridge Avenue, Evanston, Illinois 60208.

Urbanus, ed. Peter Drizhal. P.O. Box 192921, San Francisco, California 94119-2921.

Verse, eds. Brian Henry and Nancy Schoenberger. P.O. Box 8795, English Department, College of William and Mary, Williamsburg, Virginia 23187-8795.

The World, ed. Lewis Warsh. The Poetry Project, St. Mark's Church-in-the-Bowery, 131 East 10th Street, New York, New York 10003.

ACKNOWLEDGMENTS

The series editor wishes to acknowledge with thanks the assistance and support he received from Maggie Nelson and Prathima Christadas. Thanks are due as well to Glen Hartley of Writers' Representatives, and to Gillian Blake, Hamilton Cain, Jennifer Chen, Erich Hobbing, and Giulia Melucci of Scribner.

Grateful acknowledgment is made to the publications from which the poems in this volume were chosen. Unless specifically noted otherwise, copyright of the poems is held by the individual poets.

Ai: "Back in the World" appeared in *Quarterly West*. Reprinted by permission of the poet.

Sherman Alexie: "The Exaggeration of Despair" appeared in *Urbanus*. Reprinted by permission of the poet.

Agha Shahid Ali: "Return to Harmony 3" appeared in *Verse*. Reprinted by permission of the poet.

A. R. Ammons: "Strip" appeared in *The Paris Review*. Reprinted by permission of the poet.

Nin Andrews: "That Cold Summer" appeared in *Ploughshares*. Reprinted by permission of the poet.

L. S. Asekoff: "Rounding the Horn" appeared in *The American Poetry Review*. Reprinted by permission of the poet.

John Ashbery: "The Problem of Anxiety" from *Can You Hear, Bird* by John Ashbery. Copyright © 1995 by John Ashbery. Reprinted by permission of Farrar, Straus & Giroux, Inc. Originally appeared in *Arshile*.

Marianne Boruch: "Camouflage" appeared in *Shenandoah*. Reprinted by permission of the poet.

Catherine Bowman: "No Sorry" appeared in *TriQuarterly*. Reprinted by permission of the poet.

Joseph Brodsky: "Love Song" from *So Forth* by Joseph Brodsky. Copyright © 1996 by the Estate of Joseph Brodsky. Reprinted by permission of Farrar, Straus & Giroux. Originally appeared in *The New Republic*.

Stephanie Brown: "Feminine Intuition" appeared in *The American Poetry Review*. Reprinted by permission of the poet.

Joshua Clover: "The Map Room" appeared in *Iowa Review*. Reprinted by permission of the poet.

Billy Collins: "Lines Lost Among Trees" first appeared in *Poetry*, copyright © June 1996 by Billy Collins. Reprinted by permission of the Editor of *Poetry*.

Gillian Conoley: "The Sky Drank In" appeared in *American Letters and Commentary*. Reprinted by permission of the poet.

CUMULATIVE SERIES INDEX

The following are the annual listings in alphabetical order of poets and poems reprinted in the first nine editions of *The Best American Poetry*.

1988
Edited and Introduced by John Ashbery

1989
Edited and Introduced by Donald Hall

1990
Edited and Introduced by Jorie Graham

1991
Edited and Introduced by Mark Strand

1993
Edited and Introduced by Louise Glück

1994
Edited and Introduced by A. R. Ammons

1995
Edited and Introduced by Richard Howard

1996
Edited and Introduced by Adrienne Rich

ALSO AVAILABLE FROM
THE BEST AMERICAN POETRY SERIES

0-02-069846-1   THE BEST AMERICAN POETRY 1993
Edited by Louise Glück

0-671-89948-1   THE BEST AMERICAN POETRY 1994
Edited by A. R. Ammons

0-684-80151-5   THE BEST AMERICAN POETRY 1995
Edited by Richard Howard

0-684-81451-X   THE BEST AMERICAN POETRY 1996
Edited by Adrienne Rich